PRAISE FOR

CECE WINANS

"CeCe's the only woman I really want to sing with."

—Whitney Houston

"I love singing with CeCe. . . . She brings her own style and emotion to whatever she's singing."

—Patti LaBelle

"She's a very classy lady."

—Sinbad

"Ever since I've heard her sing with her brother, it's been incredible."

—Stevie Wonder

"What a great voice!"

—Regis Philbin

"I've been a fan of yours for so long. . . . You are the best!"

—Rosie O'Donnell

"It's a privilege just to be in the business with a person like CeCe because she's so real."

—Salt-N-Pepa

On a Positive Note

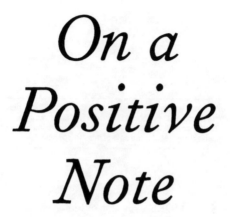

CeCe Winans
with Renita J. Weems

Her Joyous Faith,
Her Life in Music, and
Her Everyday Blessings

POCKET BOOKS

NEW YORK LONDON TORONTO SYDNEY SINGAPORE

POCKET BOOKS, a division of Simon & Schuster Inc.
1230 Avenue of the Americas, New York, NY 10020

Copyright © 1999 by Priscilla Love

Originally published in hardcover in 1999 by Pocket Books

All rights reserved, including the right to reproduce
this book or portions thereof in any form whatsoever.
For information address Pocket Books, 1230 Avenue
of the Americas, New York, NY 10020

ISBN: 0-671-02001-3

First Pocket Books trade paperback printing August 2000

10 9 8 7 6 5 4 3 2 1

POCKET and colophon are registered trademarks of
Simon & Schuster Inc.

Cover design by Brigid Pearson
Front cover photo by David Sharpe

Printed in the U.S.A.

I wish to dedicate this book to my Lord and Savior,
Jesus Christ, who is the author and finisher of my faith.

To all God's people, all the pastors and mothers who have
nurtured me, and to all my brothers and sisters in Christ who
have prayed for me and supported me every step of the way.

I love you all, and thank you so much for loving me.

Acknowledgments

$\mathcal{W}$ith my whole heart I give honor first to the Lord for His many blessings, beginning with giving me a family that loves me, friends who have stood by me, a musical talent that has disciplined me, and opportunities to sing that keep me forever grateful to God.

Writing this book would not have been possible without the aid and support of some very important people whom I wish to thank publicly and profusely.

I am blessed to have grown up in a loving, spiritual, and musical family. My parents, David and Delores Winans, provided for me and my nine siblings the God-given purposes of being musicians and artists. I want to thank them for giving me blessed memories from which to draw on in writing this book and in sharing the principles of my life.

My seven brothers and two sisters have seen to it that I had plenty of hilarious, love-filled stories to pick from when I had to describe the love and happiness that characterized the Winans household, and I am grateful to each one of them for the way in which even in adulthood we continue to love and pace each other toward excellence in our work as Christian artists. David, Ronald, Marvin, Carvin, Michael, Daniel, BeBe, Angelique, Debbie: thank you, guys.

I am truly blessed to have a husband, Alvin Love II, who loves me and supports me and two wonderful children, Alvin III and Ashley, who keep me humble and with my feet completely on the ground. I am particulary grateful to my husband of fourteen years, who continues to encourage me when I am doubtful and stand by me in love through the highs and lows of my career. My husband and children will always come first in my life, and without their patience and support I could not juggle my many roles as wife, mother, performing artist, spokeswoman, businesswoman, and now writer.

My assistant, Chandra Brooks, continues to be the administrative wind beneath my wings when I am working against deadlines, helping me to keep all the balls in the air with poise, tracking down information and details that, given my schedule, easily escape my attention. Thank you, Chandra, for all your help, including typing me through this venture.

My literary agent, Denise Stinson, worked hard to bring together all the bits and pieces involved in this writing project, and I am grateful to her for working behind the scenes in large and small ways on my behalf.

Special thanks to Renita Weems for helping me to shape my thoughts and helping me to paint the story of my journey as a Christian performing artist.

My editor, Mitch Ivers, encouraged and supported me so that I could write the book I wanted to write. In fact, my entire Pocket Books team, especially Emily Bestler and Laura Mullen, worked diligently with me in creating a product we all could be proud of.

Richard Manson is a jewel in the way he continues to support my career, my vision.

My thanks to Bill Carpenter, for always being willing and ready to help, and to Yvonne Lamb, for getting me started.

To God be the glory for the great and wonderful people He continues to send into my life as I strive to be all that He wants me to be.

Contents

Introduction
xiii

Contents

Introduction

...whatsoever things are true, whatsoever things are
honest, whatsoever things are just, whatsoever things are
pure, whatsoever things are lovely, whatsoever things
are of good report; if there be any virtue and if there be
any praise, think on these things.
—Phil. 4:8

*W*hen the song is over, the
mikes turned off, the lights dimmed, all the glitter and glamour shed, and I am left alone with my own thoughts, free to
contemplate the paths that led me to where I am today, I
pause to give thanks. I did not get here alone. I thank God for
the many people He sent in my life to carry me through each
part of my journey on the wings of love, prayer, and support.
In the shadows of every song I sing and behind every award I
garner are people who have helped me along the way. Chief

among them are my parents, David and Delores Winans, who raised me in a God-fearing home and passed on to all ten of their children a love for spiritual music, positive lyrics, and an inspirational message. Music is best when it takes your mind off what is wrong with life and reminds you of the miracle, beauty, and joy of life. A love for family, a belief in God, and a willingness to step out on faith have helped to bring me to where I am today. Many times as an adult I've pictured myself back in my parents' home in Detroit, singing while accompanied by an old upright piano, surrounded by my nine talented, raucous, musically talented brothers and sisters, who are nudging me to sing my best. I owe so much of who I am today to the habits of the heart my family instilled in me as a child, habits that I work diligently to uphold in my work as a performer and work hard to share in my relationship with my very loving husband, Alvin Love II and with my two wonderful children, Alvin III and Ashley.

I can't help it. I have always preferred to focus on the good, the positive, the blessings, the possibilities, the strength gained after the struggle, the silver lining in the cloud. That explains at least in part why I sing the kind of music I sing, despite offers to make more money singing other kinds of music. I sing to encourage people to keep the faith and focus on everything that is good, sane, and positive about life. Parts of me would wither away if I gave myself over to singing about such things as hopelessness, betrayal, despair, or desperation. This is not to say that I have not had my share of difficult and painful struggles as an artist and a young woman—I have had plenty—but I guess I am one of the blessed ones. The good times have outnumbered the bad times, and laughter has outlasted tears. In every situation, I *choose* life.

On a Positive Note is more than the story of my life; it is a celebration of life, a testimony to my lifelong commitment to sing God's glory and dwell on the positive in every situation. At thirty-four years old I haven't lived long enough to know everything about life, nor have I lived through enough to presume to tell others how to live their own lives. But I have lived long enough and through enough as a performer, wife, mother, daughter, and friend to have learned that with God's grace, you can face anything—including the uncertainties of tomorrow. *On a Positive Note* draws on some of the details of my life as a woman and performer to point to some of the lessons I have learned from life that help keep me spiritually centered and focused.

Above all I am grateful that I learned to pray at an early age. Without the discipline of prayer I could not have survived being a performer and trying to juggle the demands of my career with the challenges of being a wife and mother. I pray before every song, and I try to pray after every performance. I pray that God will get the glory out of everything I sing, do, and say, and I pray in order not to lose sight as a performer and recording artist of what is really important in life:

family, love, faith, joy, and wholeness. Prayer centers me and helps me always to remember the true source of my strength and my blessings, namely God the Creator. In fact, an abiding belief in God's grace has been my true walking cane to spiritual peace, teaching me to lean on the divine, leading me to search for the good in life. This book is a meditation on a few of the private lessons I have learned in growing up, growing older, and growing into my purpose.

Oh God

Oh God, You're wonderful, You're all-knowing, You
have all power. I love You for who You are and for all
You've done.

Oh God, You created the universe and every living
thing for Your pleasure. Life is Your gift to man and
You are the only one who can teach how to live life to its
fullness.

Oh God, I love life and I love love. I've been blessed to
know You in a very real way. It is because of You I live
a positive song. It is because of You I have this
opportunity to share my blessings with others in this
positive note.

Oh God, I draw strength from my past to make it through each day. The lessons I'm learning now will take me through my future.

Oh God, I am so blessed because You've been with me since the beginning. Before the foundations of the world You knew me, cared for and loved me. You knew my faults, failures, all the mistakes I would make and You loved me still.

Oh God, my prayer is that You stay with me, use me to spread Your positively powerful message of love throughout the world.

Oh God, keep me under the shadow of Your wings through eternity. You are Alpha and Omega, the Beginning and the End, the First and the Last. You're the Truth and the Light, You're my joy, my peace, my healer, my Father, and my Best Friend.

Oh God, You're Great!!

On a
Positive
Note

❧ ❧

1

Home Training

❧❧

Train up a child in the way he should go,
and when he is old he will not depart from it.
—Prov. 22:6

$\mathcal{W}$hen the doctor announced that my mother had given birth to a bouncing baby girl, my mother lifted her head up from her pillow and asked the attending physician, "Did you say it's a girl?" The doctor nodded. "Did you say it's a girl?" He answered affirmatively. "Did you say a girl?" Poor thing couldn't believe her ears. "Thank you, Jesus," she whispered leaning back on her pillow. "You finally came," she later told me. I was also my father's little princess. The date was October 8, 1964, and David and Delores Winans were filled with joy. Mom was especially happy because she could finally put to use the girl's name she had chosen sometime before: Priscilla, which to her meant calm, quiet, soft.

For a while it seemed as if Mom wouldn't ever get the chance to use such a pretty name. With seven high-spirited boys underfoot, Mom tried not to get her hopes up when she discovered that she was pregnant an eighth time. In those days before sonograms became a routine part of the prenatal examination, mothers and fathers had to wait until they got to the delivery room to find out the sex of their child. But the old women in the church had their own down-home ways for predicting the sex of the unborn: "Judging from the way that baby is sitting up high in your belly," they would say, "it's sho' to be a girl this time, Delores." But Mama was scared to hope. From where she looked it seemed to her that she'd carried all her babies the same: big and wide. A boy's name was already picked out. But the name Priscilla was secretly pinned to her heart . . . *just in case.*

Although Mom decided on Priscilla as her name for me, her first baby girl, as far back as my childhood days I have been known to family and friends as "CeCe." With as many siblings as I have, you'd think that someone would remember where the name CeCe came from, but no one does. As best as any of us can figure it out, my father's mother, Laura Howze, was the one to start the family tradition of calling me Sister, in honor of my position as the first girl in the family. The names Priscilla and Sister were much too dainty for my brothers' macho tastes. So Sister finally metamorphosed to "CeCe," probably because of my brothers' aversion to prissy words and Mom's tendency to shorten her children's names to something quicker to say in a fit of anger: "Peanut! Butch! Skippy! BeBe! CeCe!" If I shared some of the other family names here, however, I could be banned from the family. "CeCe" eventually stuck in everyone's memory, including Mom's. With ten children soon underfoot, she was content just to get the name CeCe out when it was time to bathe each of us and get us to bed at night.

ॐ ॐ

Only those who are really close to me know the real CeCe: the quiet, reflective, bashful, I-don't-want-to be-out-front girl from Detroit. Friends back home are surprised by the confident, outspoken CeCe who appears onstage when they compare her with the little Priscilla they recall always looking on bashfully. Even I sometimes have a hard time reconciling the two women. They're not different people, however. They're different sides of the same *me*.

There's the artist I've evolved into, the woman who is not only out front, but also singing alone, onstage, donning the latest fashions and glamorous in her makeup, making decisions (with God's help), pushing the boundaries—and *enjoying it*. Then there's the me whose idea of a good time is plopping down in the middle of my bed on a Saturday afternoon in sweats and a T-shirt, surrounded by my husband, Alvin, and our two kids, Alvin III and Ashley: Alvin II reading the business section of the newspaper on one side; the kids at the foot of the bed flipping cable channels and arguing about what each wants to see and whose turn it is to give in; and me with some devotional or daily meditation in my lap, wearing earphones and listening to the sounds of soft music and ocean waves. There's bound to be a bag of hot buttery popcorn plopped down in the middle of the bed, spilling onto the covers each time one of us readjusts our weight.

I guess there's *at least* two sides to everyone. I'm just grateful that I've finally learned to embrace both sides of me. It took me a while, however. It took me learning to be myself.

❧ ❧

For almost four years I was the sole girl among a litter of seven brothers, the different child. Growing up a girl in a house of seven brothers will make you become either aggressive and outspoken or quiet and retiring. You learn how to fight and tussle one of them to the floor, pin him down, or knee him until he gives up and cries "uncle." That's how you win the respect of a whole litter of brothers. But if you're like me and you're too small and smart to try tackling boys twice your size, you learn how to keep to yourself and play by yourself. For stimulation you learn how to create your own private inner world of fun, frolic, and friendship and not depend on the wild games boys play. My brothers were always getting into trouble, jumping up and down on the beds, wrestling one another to the mat, fighting. But I was apt to withdraw into some private corner of a room, creating imaginary worlds for myself. With the birth of my sisters, Angelique and Debbie, years later I gained playmates and soul mates, but until they were old enough to climb out of their cribs and crawl over to play with me I had to content myself with playing alone with my dolls. My macho brothers wouldn't be caught dead playing dolls with a girl.

My doll time became my quiet and creative time. Sitting in a corner of a room, alone at a table with my dolls, dressing and undressing them, styling their hair in hairstyles I'd seen worn by movie stars and glamorous singers on television, kept me occupied for hours on end. I could lose myself in my play. From time to time my brother Ronald, the second oldest of my brothers, would have pity on me and wander over to keep me company. Of all my brothers Ronald was the only one who took time out and played with my dolls and me. I can still recall him pretending to sip tea with me and my dolls, with hands large enough to clutch a football but soft enough to cuddle a doll. Ronald is the one who came up with the idea of coloring my dolls' hair with shoe polish when he noticed me struggling to design new hairstyles for my dolls. Soon, with Ronald's help, every doll had red hair. The next day every doll had black hair. The next day white hair. I was grateful to my big brother for showing me how to change the color of my dolls' hair, but I had to use my own imagination to think of ways to change their lives. With each change of hair color came the opportunity for me to create a new attitude and personality for my dolls.

When Angelique and Debbie came along, four and six years later, I was thrilled to have sisters for company, but our numbers weren't large enough to make us a formidable gang against seven brothers. Nevertheless, three proved a large enough number to tackle one of the boys if he dared stray into our domain or dared to decapitate one of our dolls. But even with two younger sisters on my side, I still felt different: old, mature, wise beyond my years. With two sisters below me and seven brothers above me, I felt squeezed in the middle with the responsibility to be mature. Those two girls were looking to me as an example, and those seven brothers were looking down at me, testing my strength and my resolve. As the older girl I usually managed to earn Angie's and Debbie's respect pretty easily. But my brothers enjoyed reducing me to tears with their constant razzing and name calling.

My sisters' births brought the Winans clan to ten children: David, Ronald, Marvin, Carvin, Michael, Daniel, Benjamin, Priscilla, Angelique, and Debbie. "I'd only planned to have two children," Mom never tires of reminding us, "a boy and a girl. It's just that the girl was slow in coming." The truth is that Mom and Dad were products of a very strict conservative religious upbringing, which frowned upon birth control and took literally the scriptures that admonish us to "multiply and replenish the earth."

Having ten children was unplanned, but the ten children were not unwanted. As each child came along, each one more of a surprise than the one before, Mom and Dad made the adjustments in their hearts and in their living space to accommodate the fruit of their love. Although there were times when they didn't know how they were going to feed another child and where they would put the child, they were confident that God would make a way. And they were right. God made a way. *"How come you have ten children, if you only meant to have two children?"* one of us was always asking them. "Evidently, God had His own plans," Mom and Dad would answer back. My parents believed, like the good Pentecostalists that they were, that even the unplanned things in life can result in blessings.

I never imagined that my little gift for singing—singing to my dolls as I styled their hair, singing as I poured them tea, singing myself to sleep at night—would be the talent God would use to catapult me into the limelight. Certainly, there's much truth to the Bible's saying "Our ways are not God's ways."

One of my greatest joys has been looking back and tracing the hand of God patiently, wisely, weaving the strands of my life together.

❦ ❦

Our house was always filled with music. It was nothing for Mom to strike up a song while standing in the kitchen cooking dinner, or for Dad to line a song as he stood in the mirror on Sunday morning, shaving and readying himself for Sunday school. Singing was the way we communicated, the way we entertained ourselves, and the way we made sense of the world. With seven boys and three girls, Mom and Dad, and a steady stream of stray cats and dogs who were taken in and given away on a whim, you had to sing to get your fair share of attention.

My parents' shared love for music brought them together back in 1950 when both were members of a local singing chorale in Detroit known as the Lemon Gospel Chorus. The founder, Louise Lemon, was a gospel great who had sung back in the 1930s and 1940s with Mahalia Jackson and the Johnson Singers of Chicago. Louise Lemon inspired young people throughout Detroit with her rousing, soul-stirring musicals, and young people everywhere flocked to join her citywide gospel choir. Music brought them together, but their shared love for each other and their mutual love for God are what persuaded David and Delores Winans to join their hearts in matrimony in 1953. She was seventeen years old and played the piano; he was nineteen years old and played the saxophone. Mom had been a member of the Lemon Gospel

Chorus since she was thirteen and a member of the Good Will Youth Choir before then. She had played the piano for small storefront churches in the city since she was a girl. My father was the grandson of a Church of God in Christ pastor and loved music. For a short time, while both were members of the choir, my parents got a chance to travel and sing, if only in a limited fashion. Every Sunday afternoon, and sometimes on an evening during the week, they were somewhere across town in Detroit or somewhere across the country in Louisiana, North or South Dakota, singing at some church anniversary service, or, if they were lucky, as the opening act for some well-established recording quartet. But soon their love for each other won out over any aspirations they had to become traveling performers.

My parents passed on their love for music to their ten children, as God would have them do. Music disciplined the mind, they believed. It also nourished the soul by providing something to muse and meditate on. Just about the time other children were sitting on their parents' laps learning to talk, each of David and Delores Winans's children were sitting around learning to sing. Singing was always such a natural part of our Winans household that I never gave it much thought, and in Detroit it seemed as if everyone sang— whether or not they could sing, they did. Music was in the air. It's amazing to me to think that there are people who go for long stretches of time—days, weeks, perhaps months—

without so much as humming a tune! In the Winans house someone was always singing.

No matter how limited the space in our house we always had a piano, and it always seemed to be in need of tuning. Mom and Dad taught us gospel songs first, as a way of keeping us ten kids entertained. But then they taught us such songs like "Just a Closer Walk with Thee" and "God Has Smiled on Me" as a way of teaching us about faith and hope, and as a way of instilling reverence of and love for God in our hearts. They succeeded. Gospel music at home softened our hearts for the sermons and Sunday school lessons we would later have to listen attentively to, sitting in those hard church pews.

All seven of my brothers grew up singing: David, Ronald, Marvin, Carvin, Daniel, Michael, and Benjamin (BeBe). Some girls' brothers fix cars and excel in sports—mine sang. I can't recall the first time I heard my brothers singing—it would be easier to try to come up with times when they *weren't* singing. Those were the times when they were goofing off, cutting up, or into some mischief around the house. My older brothers were always coming up with songs; some they made up, some they learned at church. They were good about leading the family in song at special gatherings for all the family and extended family. Each brother had his own style and distinctive sound, which lent a special sound to their harmonies. Together their rich sound made you think they were angels sent from God. That's if you didn't know any better. Together their voices blended and melded and created a sound that soon would leave churches and other audiences spellbound. Their harmonies and powerful lyrics combined to make them a highly sought-after teenage quartet known in the early and mid-1970s as the Testimonials. So first the boys in the Winans family sang, and then the girls in the Winans family sang.

With ten children in the house there was always a steady drone of noise. The challenge for a quiet introverted child like me was to figure out what noise to shut out and what noise to embrace. The sound of slamming doors, clanging pots, and quarreling siblings—those were sounds I could safely ignore. The sound of Mom humming a tune from church, Dad praying in song, or one of my seven brothers banging out a tune of his own creation on the piano—those were the kinds that left my soul tingling. There was singing throughout the day and into the night. After teasing one another back and forth about whose head was shaped the funniest, who was the clumsiest, whose feet stank most from their gym shoes, and who had holes in their underwear, we'd sing ourselves to sleep. It was like a big camp. Something was always going on. Usually the last song we'd sing at night sometimes was:

"Thank You for Your love so sweet.
Thank You for the food we eat.

Thank You for the birds that sing.
Thank You God for everything . . . good night!"

❧ ❧

My parents worked hard to create a home environment in which love took priority over things. Discipline was second to love. Laughter ran a close third. We didn't have a lot of the things we wanted, but there was always more than enough of the things we needed. Mom, the soft rock of the family, with her quiet but firm ways, worked all day as a medical transcriptionist at a local hospital and came home to her second job in the evening: cooking, mending, and praying for her large brood. Always even tempered and naturally soft-spoken, she seemed always to know what to say to make the pain go away. I admired her for her calm. She had the patience of Job, as they say, but when that patience ran out she wasn't hesitant about taking things into her own hands—even if that included one of our behinds.

One thing for sure, my seven brothers were always into something. Boys always need to test their strength, prove their strength, or challenge someone else's strength. They are always fighting, about to fight, or just getting over a fight. Most of the fray in the house was around the older boys (David, Ronald, Marvin, and Carvin) ganging up against the younger ones (Michael, Daniel, and BeBe). The "top half against the bottom half" is the way they described themselves.

Fights always broke out about who drank the last bit of Kool-Aid, who broke what, who ripped whose pair of pants, or whose turn it was to sleep on the floor. My parents never knew their children fought. We laughed behind closed doors when we heard one of them boasting proudly to a friend, "Our children never fight." Boy, were they wrong. They never had a clue because, despite our differences, we all saw to it that furniture, appliances, and windows were pieced together, taped together, glued together, stuck together, or just prayed together before our parents got home. If we didn't, everyone would have to pay.

No doubt about it, Mom and Dad were strict disciplinarians. Dad's floggings were the worst, or so it seemed. My brothers' howls from the basement could be heard from every corner of the house as Dad landed his belt against their backsides. But Mom's soft manner was not to be mistaken for weakness. A short, soft, caramel-complexioned woman, with wide sloping eyes and a warm engaging smile (which I inherited), Mom wouldn't stand for any mess. She said what she meant and meant every last word that she said. She was not one to spare the rod and spoil the child. But when she whipped her ten children, it was as much to teach us discipline and self-control as it was to express her disappointment over something we'd done. Raised in a disciplined home herself, Mom was convinced of the virtues of discipline. She was determined that her children weren't going to grow up as wild puppies, which in our home meant acting as if you didn't have any home training. Above all, "home training" meant respecting your parents, respecting elders, no talking back, and having a fear of God. I learned a large part of what it means to be a parent from watching my parents teach us discipline and respect. In those early years, with seven boys to rear, Mom was forever having to whip someone, it seems. "Perhaps she'll be too tired to whip us when she gets home,"one of my brothers would wish out loud whenever a plate, a window, or knickknack had gotten broken. But if Mom was too tired to get you that day, she was sure to get you the next day. She *never* forgot. Nothing was worse than a whipping that Mom had put off for a day. No matter how much we had it coming to us, Mom was always fair. She dispatched her duty with the belt, ironing cord, shoe, or whatever was handy with more a sense of responsibility than hysterical outrage.

Being quiet and observant I took note and learned from the scoldings meted out to my siblings. Not that I was an angel. It's just that when you weighed my misdeeds against those of my siblings, I ended up *looking* like an angel.

"CeCe gets away with murder," my older brothers complained. They thought I was spoiled.

"When you came along, everything was different," Michael offered. "Stuff Mom and Dad beat us for, you got away with, scot-free."

It wasn't that I was the favorite. It's just that by the time my sisters and I came along, Mom was finally too tired to keep up the beatings. "When CeCe, Angie, and Debbie came around, I was plumb out of strength," Mom likes to say with a smile on her face. She loved her sons, but she loved having daughters even more, and it took her a long time to finally have a girl. Raised with only a sister as a sibling, Mom had a soft spot in her heart for her daughters. But not even her love for us would make her spare the rod when the time came to discipline us. My brothers only think I had it easier than they did. And I, of course, think my younger sisters had it easier than I did, that they're the ones who got away with murder. That explains why Angie and Debbie are more outspoken and daring than me. Things I only dreamed of saying and doing, they said and did and got away with.

I was more reserved than my siblings, but I was still no angel. I did my share of arguing, fighting, and breaking up things. The few whippings I do recall were always the result of my trying to hang with my brothers. One whipping stands out in particular because it emblazoned on my mind the different expectations placed on girls and boys.

Tired of being left out of my brothers' loud, boisterous games, I decided this one afternoon, after getting my hair done, that I wanted to be a part of the fun. I could hear Michael, Daniel, and BeBe playing downstairs in the basement, and Mom and Dad weren't home. Now we all knew that we weren't allowed to have water fights in the house, but that didn't stop them. I was bored that day, and I wanted to join the fun. I stopped whatever I was doing and made my way down into the basement. When my brothers saw me, my presence was met with groans and furious shakes of the head. "No way," they said. "Get outta here." I begged to be allowed in the fun. "Your hair," BeBe reminded me. My mother had paid good money to Sister Walker the beautician for me to get one of those hard presses that little black girls got back then in order for their hair to stay nice and straight for weeks. "No girls," said Daniel, not buying it. I begged and finally convinced them to let me join in.

Within a few seconds water was all over my face, and I was squealing with delight. The rules to my brothers' games were always clear: no mercy given, no mercy gotten, even to girls. Someone handed me a water bottle (a discarded bottle of Windex filled with water), and the game was on. Soon water was everywhere in the basement. I gave as good as I got, and the fun went on for what seems like hours. Everybody forgot about the time, and everybody forgot about my hair—including me. No one gave a thought about the wet puddles that were gathering around our feet. After we had finished playing, when all the water was mopped up and everything was back in place, BeBe looked over at me and yelled, "Look at your hair!" I reached up and felt my hard-pressed hair frizzing all over my head. I knew I was in trouble. Mom would be home soon. I ran upstairs to see what I could do and found some hair oil and began applying fistfuls to my hair. I took a brush and stroked my hair repeatedly to the side. By the time I heard Mom come through the door downstairs, I had begun to like what I saw in the mirror. My hair was a mass of thick, curly waves lying to the side of my face. I was so proud of the new hairstyle I'd stumbled on that I covered my head with a blanket and proceeded downstairs to show off my new do.

Don't ask me what I was thinking; I must have been out of my mind to think that my mother would be impressed by my efforts. "What are you doing, CeCe?" Daniel asked when he saw the blanket on my head. I jerked the blanket off my head and yelled, "Surprise!" Mom took one look at me, and I knew from her expression that it was over. Her eyes never left my head. "Girl, what's wrong with your head?" she screamed. She was in shock. All I could get out of my mouth was, "Michael, Daniel, and BeBe were having a water fight . . ." Before you knew it, all four of us were beaten that day. Mom beat Michael, Daniel, and BeBe because they were supposed to know better than to start a water fight in the house, even if it was in the basement. Mom beat me because I should have known better as a girl that time and money had gone into getting my hair done. I did remember, but I had completely forgotten about all those things once the water fight began. I couldn't help myself. Mom was determined to help me.

That whipping taught me many things, among them that water is the bane of little black girls' hair. It was a lesson I would have occasion to learn again and again throughout my childhood. I resented the limitations placed on black girls' fun. Boys never have to worry about what water does to their hair. From that day, I've had a love-hate relationship with hair, especially my own. I'm always fretting over it and wishing it would just let me have my way.

For all her tough discipline, what struck me most about my mother is that she told you the truth, disciplined you, and then left you with the feeling that everything was going to be all right. Give her a few hours, after her anger had subsided, and she could be heard singing some gospel tune on the other side of the house. Eventually she would find you in your room and stand in the door and give you one of her special mother looks that said, "Now, baby, you know Mommy loves you." Your heart had to soften, even if your backside still stung. I was fortunate to grow up in a very forgiving home. Neither Mom nor Dad held a grudge for very long. As quickly as their anger rose, it subsided. They disciplined you and moved on. Neither of them made us feel as though we had to beg for their love, beg for their forgiveness, or beg to be a part of the family. Love was free, but with it came responsibilities and accountability. I trusted my parents' discipline when I was a child, and I never doubted their love. They prayed for us when we were sick, and they disciplined us when we were wrong. They beat us as a way of protecting us from the things they knew awaited us as young black children, and they prayed for us, like so many black parents before and after them, asking God to save us from the things that preyed on black children, things they had no way of protecting us from.

I learned about the healing power of music from observing my parents. I would watch Mom in particular come through the door after a day's work at Metropolitan Hospital, and it seemed that the world was upon her shoulders. Nevertheless, she rarely complained. I remember her staying up all night, tired, sleepy, at her sewing machine, determined to make one of us something to wear for the next morning. I longed to make her smile and chase the sadness away. But there's some sadness only Jesus can chase away. Until then, a good song can lift the heart. We could always depend on an uplifting favorite hymn, like one my grandmother sang at church, to lift whatever cloud loomed over our hearth.

He's got better things for you,
No one on earth can do.
He's got the Holy Ghost and fire
And it sho' will make you true.

He's got better things for you,
No one on earth can do.

So place your mind on Jesus;
He's got better things for you.

As with many of the songs I heard around home, I must admit that I didn't always understand what I and others were singing about. What did I know about the Lord having better things for me? What did I know about God's amazing grace? Some of the lyrics of "Amazing Grace" (like "wretch") sounded dangerous to me. But you don't always have to understand the words in order to feel the emotions of a song. I could tell by the inflections in my mother's voice, or the way my father rocked and rejoiced during certain songs, that music had the power to transport you back or forward into secret places. Even though I didn't always understand the words, music's power to arrest the emotions was enough to make me stand in awe.

Only a quiet, easygoing temperament like Mom's could survive being married to a hyperactive, outgoing, no-one-is-a-stranger man like my father. Mom's steady spirit was the anchor that kept my father from floating right off the face of the earth. David Winans Sr., also known as Elder "Skip" Winans, never met a stranger in his life. Within just a few minutes, all strangers are bosom friends to Dad. A barber by trade, Dad wasn't above taking odd jobs in order to make ends meet. To keep food on his family's table, he worked a stream of jobs in his lifetime, from driving a taxi to selling cars. His humor kept the family laughing, and his abundant energy kept us too busy with chores and games to complain about what we lacked. Dad was the kind of man who had to be busy doing something. He was always thinking of something new. Always talking and keeping things going. If Mom was always a steady source of support and strength for us kids, Dad was our motivator and inspiration. He was always one dream ahead of the rest of us. Although he was an elder in the church and his grandfather founded the church he had grown up in, Mack Avenue Church of God in Christ, Dad never felt any calling from God to pastor a church. Dad used his talents for ministry in inspiring others and motivating us kids to be our best. He always had to be active, moving, and doing.

When one of us complained about being bored or that we didn't have anyone to play with, he would remind us that there were ten of us: "You get tired of playing with one sister or brother, there's always another child in this house you can play with." Laughter was often Dad's best tool for inspiring and encouraging others, and no matter how tight things got at home he would never let us wallow in what we didn't have. Even the most difficult times could be laughed at. "There were times we were so poor, I opened up the icebox and all I saw was a light," he loved to tell everyone. Both of my parents, being very godly people, set down strict rules that outlawed dancing, parties, makeup, and movie going, but still I credit both of them with enormous wisdom.

Dad in particular never lost sight of the fact that we were young and needed something to do. He was always coming up with something for us (and himself!) to do. He showed us that a saved life was not a bored life. When we weren't bowling, we were skating. When we weren't skating, we were playing baseball or running track. If we weren't playing sports, we were having concerts. Dad was always organizing something for youth: youth at church and youth in our neighborhood. You'd think that he had enough kids of his own and wouldn't want to be bothered with any more, but Dad has always been young at heart.

As far as Dad was concerned, there was always room in the Winanses' house for one more child. Kids from the neighborhood and from church were always dropping by and hanging out at our place. They often came under the pretense of hanging out with my brothers, but most of the times they just wanted to see what Dad was up to—they wanted to challenge him to a game of ball, listen to him talk, or have him tell one of his funny stories that left them laughing and feeling better about life. Dad inherited his wit and humor from his mother, Grandmother Howze, and remains one of the funniest men I know.

As poor as we were, with ten children to clothe and feed, Dad was always finding money to organize teams—baseball, bowling, track teams, anything to keep us young people occupied. Dad always made sure that there was always *something*

for us to do. He encouraged each of us to achieve our potential, then to reach further, and always to trust God. Even
though Dad had to work two, sometimes three jobs in order to
keep food on the table, even though there was never enough
money to go around, Dad kept us motivated to take our minds
off what we *didn't* have and to thank God for the things we *did*
have: each other, our love, our faith, and our rich legacy as
Winanses.

ᔕᔕ ᔕᔕ

The house on Woodingham and Seven Mile, where my
parents moved their family of what at the time were eight
children, will always be home to me. My older brothers have
their own memories of living and growing up in the projects
of Detroit, where life was harsher and space was cramped,
but those are not my memories. By the time I was born, my
parents had scraped and saved enough money to move their
expanding family to safer and better quarters, in a little
framed house in West Detroit. Of all the places I've lived,
that house is where my memories of what it means to be safe
and happy were first formed. By anyone's standards, there's
nothing breathtaking about the house: it's your typical brick,
two-story home built just after World War II, neither grand
nor spectacular, but it was wanted. In fact, the one thing it
had going for it was the fact that David and Delores Winans
wanted it so deeply for what would eventually be their family

of twelve. With many of their friends living in the projects and in small apartments my parents felt blessed to be able to find a single-family dwelling they could afford. What more could any house ask for than that it be appreciated by its owners. In exchange for appreciation and gratitude, even a modest house will do what it can to make its inhabitants feel at home.

With three bedrooms, a basement, and one and a half baths, our Woodingham home gave us more space than a lot of other people had: one bedroom for the girls, one bedroom for the boys, and a bedroom for Mom and Dad. I drive through the old neighborhood now when I go back home, and I wonder how in the world my parents managed to raise ten children in that little brown brick house with the tiny, tiny lawn. I know their answer without asking, "Only with the help of God." Company was always dropping by, someone was always dashing in and slamming the door in a rush to get to the bathroom, someone was always out playing ball in the yard, someone was always knocking on the door bumming a ride to church. The house was often filled with friends, classmates, extended family—as though ten children were not enough. There wasn't enough room for anyone to have privacy, but there was always enough room for one more. With seven boys in one bedroom, my brothers took turns sleeping on the floor. That's the way it was done—not only at our house but at every other black or working-class home I knew where there were more children than there were beds. It didn't seem strange back then to us. Fighting each night for your turn to sleep in one of the bunk beds was a way of life. If you lost the fight or if you showed up late for bed, you slept on the floor—period. The three of us girls had it easier, with a queen-size bed between us, but when it came to twelve people trying to get into one and a half bathrooms, it was every boy and girl, and man and woman, for himself and herself. Still, with all the laughter, love, and singing that took place at 19131 Woodingham, no one thought to equate a shortage of space with a shortage of happiness. One simply had nothing to do with the other. That distinction was one that Mom and Dad made sure was stamped on our minds, and I'm glad they did. Now that I'm older I've learned that Mom and Dad were right: just because you live in a big fancy house doesn't mean you're happy. It might just mean that you have more rooms in which to be miserable and lonely. I look at the home in which I now live—with its big, spacious rooms, high ceilings, and state-of-the-art technology—and I know that I can't afford to equate luxury with happiness. I thank God for all the comfort, believe me, but I also thank God that long before I found comfort in large living spaces, I embarked on a path to find peace of mind through prayer, song, and laughter within my soul.

❧ ❧

There were so many things that we didn't have when I was growing up, but at the same time, there were so many other things that we had in abundance: we had one another, we had music, we had parents who loved us, we had family and friends who surrounded us with their prayers, and we had parents and grandparents who were always around to guide us. We had memories in the making. For instance, my father's mother, Grandmother Howze, was a positive influence and my very best friend. She was my girl, and I was hers. One of the things I loved most about Grandmother Howze was that she never tired of me. She was the kind of grandmother every bashful girl needs in her life: someone old and patient enough to see beyond a child's misguided questions to her hungry heart on the other side. "God's got His hands on you, CeCe. Just keep your hands in His hands, and you'll be all right." I loved my grandmother's wisdom, and I loved to be around her. She simply had it going on. She was short and golden brown with long beautiful salt-and-pepper hair that she always wore in a bun. (I remember wondering as a child why Grandmother Howze would never wear her beautiful hair down.) She looked and spoke as though she knew more than she was telling. But she always told you just enough to keep you coming back for more. She had an infectious laugh, and when she cried her eyes twinkled as she spoke to you. She was one of the funniest people I knew, full of wisdom, wit, and gaiety. For instance, she was always buying things to help Mom and Dad out with their ten children. One time she bought an industrial-size box of toilet paper for the family, clearly expecting it to last several months, only to discover that it was gone after a few short weeks. Grandmother Howze, who'd only had one child to raise, my father, was shocked to discover how quickly a family of twelve goes through an industrial size box of toilet paper. "Y'all act like you have two butts a piece!" she replied.

Grandmother Howze kept us laughing. She knew how to make a joke out of poverty, sickness, fights, and even heartache. She taught me things that have stayed with me for a lifetime, things I try to pass on to my own children and try to impart in my music: peace, wisdom, joy, and hope.

My most vivid memories of my father's mother are much greater than the many *things* she gave me: the toys, the money, the trips across the city, and the favorite foods she cooked just for me, whom she called "Sister," her first and oldest granddaughter: And my, my, my, Grandmother Howze could cook! What I remember above all is her spirit, the power she possessed in her very presence. So convinced was I of her powers that I loved following her around. The only house where my father allowed me to stay overnight was hers. I especially enjoyed sitting around with her and the other older women in the church, listening to them regale one another with stories of their days as younger women, their dreams for their children, and their faith in God. Convinced that my grandmother was the most special person in the whole world, I was certain that her prayers got through to God quicker because only her prayers managed to make the stomach pains I chronically suffered as a child as a result of a hernia disappear. She was definitely the only person who could calm my dad. Grandmother Howze brought peace wherever she went. If things were in an uproar in our house—my brothers fighting, Mom and Dad disagreeing on a matter, or if things were just plain out of sorts—we knew whom to call. When Grandmother Howze approached, the spirit of peace and calm would fall. It's the part of her soul that I've tried to take with me wherever I am. Whenever I'm home, surrounded by ringing phones, humming fax machines, ringing doorbells, arguing children in the background, or whenever I'm in the car trying to make a dash to the airport in rush-hour traffic to make it to the West Coast for an evening awards dinner, or whenever I'm in the studio for ten hours working with producers and musicians who are uptight about our twelfth take on the same song, I try to recall Grandmother Howze's calm. I don't always succeed, but I try. I pray for that inner peace that transcends all understanding. I want my husband and children to remember me the way I remember Grandmother Howze, namely that when I walk through the door, the family can breathe a sigh of relief, not because of what I hold in my hands but because of what I bring in my heart.

I thought my grandmother would be with me forever. But that was the wish of an adoring granddaughter. In those final days of her battle with cancer, when it became clear that she couldn't take care of herself, God did exactly what she had wanted and prayed all along: she hoped God would spare her family the toil of caring for a dying old woman and would take her quickly on home with Him. She lived to see my marriage to a man she approved of greatly, and she was the only one who suspected that my flu symptoms were those of pregnancy, still she died before she had a chance to see my career take off and before she had a chance to get to know my children. I know she would have added richness to all our lives. But when I saw her beginning to decline before my eyes I prayed with her that God would heal her or take her home. As much as it hurts years later to say this, I'm glad God heeded our prayers. I'm glad God took her home, where she could witness the progression of my life and career from a better, safer vantage point.

❧ ❧

What I learned from those very early formative years in my parents' house, surrounded by my parents, brothers and sisters, and grandparents was that not all blessings can be touched, stroked, and clutched with the hand. Some blessings must be experienced only with the heart. The love of parents, the warmth and laughter of brothers and sisters, the special companionship of a big brother who stoops to enter the world of his little sister and sip tea with her and her dolls, the gift of music to inspire the soul, and special time with a grandmother who gives presents from the heart are part of those intangible tokens of God's grace that stay with you a lifetime, filling you with memories of love, security, hope, and possibilities.

Home and Family

Blessed quietness, peace and rest,
Noisy, crowded and being surrounded by people you love
    is simply the best.
A safe environment, my refuge, my house was my
    hiding place,
A solid foundation. I could stand on Godly principles,
    and the teachings of God's grace.

Home and family, two gifts often taken for granted,
But Lord, I'm thankful and grateful for them both.
You have shown me your love abundantly,
I am blessed to have precious memories of home and
    family.

2

Fill My Cup

Blessed are those who hunger and thirst for
righteousness, for they shall be filled.
—*Matt. 5:6*

*C*hurch was my family's second home. None of us complained much about it—not that it would have done any good. We *had* to go. David and Delores wouldn't hear of our not going. Fortunately for us, church was cool. Our friends were there, our hearts were there, and our identity as a God-fearing family was there.

Most importantly, church was the only place to try out our stuff as young people, the only place our parents permitted us to hang out. We flirted, we courted, we tried out new hairstyles, honed our skills, and tested our talents—all at church. It was a wonderful place to be. The Winans children had to *be* there all the time. When we weren't at church service on Tuesday, Friday, and Sunday, we were attending summer church camps, going to revivals, or off somewhere either singing or rehearsing in the young people's choir.

Every child in the church had to join the children's choir, whether you could sing or not. Adults could choose whether or not they wanted to join the adult choirs, but for children it was a given. The choir was the primary ministry to youth in the church, and parents saw to it that their kids went and joined the church's choir for the same reason they saw to it that they attended public school: it was the law, an unspoken law in the church buoyed by the biblical injunction "Let everything that has breath praise the Lord." There was no better place for children to learn discipline, poise, confidence, and teamwork than in the church's youth choir. Choir wasn't just a place for children whose parents hoped they would grow up to be great singers. For adults in my church it was important for children to grow up with sacred skills and core values. Choir was a place where children could learn to work with others in a team effort while simultaneously learning the godly principles of faith, prayer, and holiness. "Sit up," "Smile," "Sing like you mean it," "Before you sing, pray," "Sing for Jesus," "If you don't show up to rehearse, don't show up to sing," or "If you don't feel it, the audience won't feel it." "Don't open your mouth until you see the sign to open your mouth." "Take that gum out of your mouth." These admonitions instilled in me the discipline and poise I would need years later when singing was much more than a way of staying out of trouble.

Church became a safe haven for me, a place where I was surrounded by God-fearing people: preachers, mothers, deacons, trustees, friends, and family. Church was my family, which explains why we called everyone "Sister So-and So" or "Brother So-and-So" or "Mother So-and-So." Anyone could discipline anyone else's child. We loved one another as family, and we were taught that we were responsible for one another's nurturance and care. The adults felt responsible for one another's children. Mother So-and-So had as much right to whip one of us as did our own parents, no permission needed, no talking back allowed.

I appreciated being surrounded by that kind of love. When someone was sick in a family, the whole church rallied together to take turns at the hospital visiting the sick, taking food to the home of the afflicted family member, coming over to the home and offering to cook, clean, or take care of the rest of the children. When one person lost a job, the church pitched in and did what it could to help the family. When there was a death in a family, we all mourned and did what we could to lighten the load of the bereaved.

While my mother was raised in the Baptist church, my father's roots are deep in the Church of God in Christ. The denomination originated in 1907 when Charles H. Mason first joined a small body of Baptist ministers who were seeking a greater spiritual involvement than the Baptists offered. He eventually attended the Azusa Street Revival in Los Angeles in 1907 with a small band of holiness believers and remained at Azusa for approximately five weeks, speaking in tongues and receiving the Holy Ghost. Mason later settled in Memphis, where he began a series of services that attracted a large following of people, and these services eventually led to the founding of the Church of God in Christ. My father's grandfather first met with Mason's holiness teaching there in Memphis in the 1920s as he was making his way up from Belvonia, Mississippi, where he and his family had been sharecroppers. They were on their way out of Mississippi because one of his sons had been threatened with a whipping by one of the white landowners. Great-grandfather Isaiah was greatly impressed with the fiery teachings of the Church of God in Christ, accepted his call to preach there under Mason, and promised Mason to help plant Church of God in Christ churches in Michigan when he got up north. When Isaiah Winans got to Michigan his first order of business was to start the Zion Congregational Church of God in Christ, which later came to be known as the Mack Avenue Church of God in Christ. It was there in my great-grandfather's church that three generations of Winans were spiritually shaped and cared for.

My father's mother, Laura, and father, Carvin, were not married when Laura became pregnant with my father, David. But Laura's mother saw to it that my father was raised at Mack Avenue Church with his father around and his grandfather as his pastor. My father grew up around his father but had very little to do with him, and my father carried his mother's name, Glenn. Twenty-nine years later, when my father was married with seven sons, Great-grandfather Isaiah recognized that there were no male Winans to carry on the family name and asked my father to change his name to Winans. My father consented. "Despite the fact that for years my father denied I was his child," my father tells, "when my grandfather, the man who'd taught me as my pastor everything I knew about the Lord and forgiveness, when he asked me to take his name, Winans, as my own, my heart couldn't help but melt with forgiveness. I couldn't block the blessings due to my family because of what my mother and father did not do. Winans was my family name, and it was my grandfather's vision that this family would one day be a blessing to the church of Christ." My own most poignant memories of what it means to belong to a family, a church family, and a spiritual village were shaped there at the church founded by my great-grandfather Isaiah Winans. Although he died a couple of years after I was born, he lived long enough to see his family united together in love: his son, his only grandson (my father), and his great-grandsons (my seven brothers) worshiping as Winans in his church. Love and forgiveness, my father learned through him, are essential to keeping a family together.

⚮ ⚮

Some of my fondest memories of church involve food: fried chicken, macaroni and cheese, homemade rolls, dressing, gravy, green string beans, and ice cream for dessert were all a standard part of the feast served in the fellowship hall every Sunday after church. If we made it to Sunday school, we got a chance to have church breakfast: fried chicken, rice and gravy, and homemade biscuits. (No wonder I'm still fighting the battle of the bulge in my thirties.) The great food and great people made church a wonderful and safe place for me as a child.

Despite the hell-fire-and-brimstone message of some of the sermons of Elder Stacks, our pastor, I always looked forward to going to church. The pastor's climax at the end of his sermon—"Heaven or hell!"—never made me flinch from God; it had the curious effect of making me draw closer. With all the sensitivities and sincerity of a child, I desperately wanted to please God and always felt that I missed the mark. Every Sunday, with all the earnestness of my six-year-old heart I always made my way to the altar during service to ask God to search my heart. I didn't want to go to hell, and I didn't want to displease God. I only wanted what God wanted for me.

Church, Church

Hallelujah, Hallelujah,
What an exciting place to me.
Glory to God, glory to God,
I was blind but now I see.
Praise the Lord, praise the Lord,
Everyone in bondage can be set free.
Thank you Jesus, thank you Jesus,
You are the Lord of Lords, and the Prince of Peace.

❧ ❧

Given my deep roots in the Holiness church, it should come as no surprise that only one kind of music was permitted in David and Delores's home: gospel music. Raised in the Pentecostal tradition, my parents were determined that they would raise their children in the way of holiness and sanctification. This meant no parties, no clubs, no smoking, no drinking, no makeup, no jewelry, no finger popping, and above all no secular music. We were faithful members of my great-grandfather's Mack Avenue Church of God in Christ and later the Shalom Temple Church. Mom and Dad sang in the adult choirs on and off over the years as time and their work permitted, and Mom from time to time played the piano for some of the choirs. Both parents threatened to brand us if they ever caught us playing "worldly music" in the house or even in the car. "Holiness or hell" was the way they put it.

Holiness was the way it was going to be in the Winans home.

But you can't possibly live in Detroit, the Motor City, home to Motown, and not hear what in religious circles goes by the name of secular or worldly music. Pop and rhythm and blues are part of the very molecules that make up Detroit's air. While none of us kids dared to play secular music in the home, I can't say that we remained totally ignorant of the music in the streets. You couldn't help hearing it. Walking across the school yard or down to the corner store, we heard the sounds of the Four Tops, Stevie Wonder, Marvin Gaye, the Supremes, Jackson 5, Gladys Knight and the Pips, or the Temptations blaring from a radio or record player. In huddles on street corners or in packs at their school lockers boys practiced the Pips' gliding moves and rehearsed the Temptations' smooth sounds, determined to imitate and coordinate the choreography and rhythms blaring from the records.

Sometimes we pretended to be Gladys Knight and the Pips with me as Gladys and Michael, Daniel, and BeBe as the Pips. Since we were Pentecostal born and bred, and David and Delores's children alive or dead, we knew better than to glide our limbs, pop our fingers, or move our hips the way we'd seen others do. Instead we rocked and swayed our bodies along the sanctified lines of famed inspirational singers such as Shirley Caesar and Andrae Crouch as we sang Gladys and the Pips' hits like "Midnight Train to Georgia" or "I Heard It through the Grapevine." Despite our Pentecostal upbringing the Winans children were as much a product of our Motown environment as were the kids who lived next door in Detroit. We inhaled the fresh melodies and let the mellow harmonies of the music on the streets run across our minds every time we were in their reach. The only difference was that we left those sounds on the street whenever we crossed the threshold of our home. We knew better than to let Mom and Dad come home and catch worldly music blasting from our radio, and no one dared to play any of those tantalizing rhythms on the family piano. Mom and Dad had ears in the back of their heads, we were certain.

The truth is that no matter how much we loved the music, we cared about what our parents thought about us, and we didn't want to do or perform anything that would bring them disrespect or shame. What struggling, black working-class families back then lacked in terms of prestige and money, parents like mine made up for in the pride they took in keeping a clean home, raising well-behaved children, and modeling decency in their community.

God's word and music taught me faith and gave me hope. It blessed me where I hurt. It healed me of my shyness and gave my life purpose. And His music brought me messages on how to triumph over life's disappointments and find happiness in ordinary moments with the ones you love. By teaching us kids to sing at an early age, Mom and Dad made sure that the noise in the Winans house would at least be melodious and purposeful. A song like "His Eye Is on the Sparrow," which we learned to sing at an early age by hearing Mom and Dad humming and singing it, inspired me to have faith in God long before I grew up to discover for myself how lonely and cold life can be: "His eye is on sparrow, and I know He's watching me." The promises that song held out—of happiness, freedom, and God's continuing presence—were irresistible to my heart.

I didn't care that religious music was the only music my parents allowed in our house. I just loved music. I loved even more what it did to my family. Music brought us together. Music gave us something to do as a family. Music took our minds off what we didn't have and reminded us of what we *did* have, which was one another. Music was my family's blessing. Gospel music gave us something positive to rehearse in our soul. There would be plenty enough time to think about betrayal, seduction, broken promises, and sensuality. My mother's tunes about God's grace and my father's prayer for God's mercy gave us inspiring things to sing about and taught us some of our most important lessons about triumph and tragedy. Music became a place in which my soul could recline.

Sister Joyce Glenn, a relative of the family and director of the children's choir at church, was the person who talked me into my first solo with the Sunshine Band. As director of the Sunshine Band choir, Sister Glenn decided which songs we sang, who would sing them, and when they would sing. According to her, I was ready at seven years old. I disagreed, I protested, I cried, I begged, and I pleaded to stay put in my front-row spot there in the Sunshine Band. I didn't want to be out front. Despite all the times I'd sat in my brothers' laps on our way back and forth to church as they practiced tune after tune for the Sunday afternoon youth concert, despite all the times I'd joined them at home singing back and forth to one another from across the expanse of our bedrooms, even though I'd had plenty of practice sitting down at the piano with one of them banging out and singing a song of our own making, I just didn't feel ready to take on such a big responsibility. Sister Glenn was not moved by the fears and tears of a seven-year-old. I was ready, she said, and my mother and father agreed. That settled it.

The church's annual convocation was the place for my debut solo. The Sunshine Band was part of the annual lineup of musical offerings, and I would sing my number. Annual convocation is a traditional gathering time in Pentecostal churches at which sister churches from all over the city, state, and district gather at a local church for a week of worship, teaching, musicals, and church business. A combination of a homecoming and a church revival, convocation at Mack Avenue Church of God in Christ was a special time for my family. Because it was the church my paternal great-grandfather had founded decades earlier, family and friends from around the state would return to Mack Avenue to renew our bonds through worship and fellowship. What better place for me to debut as a soloist, reasoned Sister Glenn and my family, than in my family church surrounded by relatives, friends, and tons of well-wishers. And though this was the logic of the adults, I thought the idea stunk.

After weeks of rehearsals, both at church and at home, the big day came. I was still trying to think of ways to get out of it, but I knew none of them would work. The sight of her first daughter, with her wide eyes and bright smile, crying and begging to be spared, didn't move my mother, and she was a compassionate woman usually moved by tears. I knew I was doomed. Even Grandmother Howze, who normally sided with me on all things, hadn't been persuaded by my protests. I knew there was no sense in trying the old gag routine. It was simpler to get it over with. Maybe, I hoped, the whole church would forget about the fact that I was supposed to sing, but that was just a frightened child's wish.

When the time came, and the pianist struck up the first chords to my solo, my heart was pounding in my ears. Moisture gathered in my palms and at the nape of my neck. How I managed to unglue myself from my seat and take the long walk to the towering gray steel mike at the front of the church, I don't know, but I did. A chorus of well wishers escorted me to the mike: "Sing, baby," " Sing CeCe." "Sing for Jesus, child." One of those voices was my father's, and he is still to this day my loudest and number one fan.

I stood at Sister Glenn's beckoning call and made my way to the microphone standing near the piano, and I could feel the fear welling in my throat. The sound of the fans blowing throughout the sanctuary, which I'd never noticed before, made me doubt that anyone would be able to hear me. I didn't know whether that was good or bad. Sister Glenn adjusted the mike for my height, and I looked at her with pleading eyes. She returned my plea with a look of loving confidence, and something in me relaxed for the first time in weeks. I closed my eyes, and as the piano started, I felt the words to the song bubble up inside me. They came so fast I had to clench my fists to keep them from spilling out of me before their time; but I couldn't keep tears from rolling down my cheeks.

"Fill my cup, Lord.
I lift it up Lord.
Come and quench this thirsting of my soul.
Bread of Heaven.
Feed me till I want no more.
Fill my cup, fill it up, and make me whole."

It wasn't a typical song for a child to sing. The deep longing it expressed escaped me at seven years old, but the image of a cup—an empty cup, an empty uplifted cup—was something with which I could identify. The taste of my own salty tears streaming down my face and into the corners of my mouth kept me present to where I was. Otherwise, I might have floated away into my own world of make-believe. The sight of me singing, crying, was too much. As I peered through my tears, I could make out people rocking, waving handkerchiefs, and rising to their feet. Some of them were crying themselves. I was just happy that it was over when it was over, but the strange warmth that came over me when I finished wasn't just relief. It was like a presence that came over me, a warm embrace from something outside of me that was at the same time something profoundly a part of me—if that makes any sense.

The song was over. But my life with music was just beginning: *my* life. Looking back on it, I know now that my own personal, individual ministry as a singer was born that day, but I didn't know it back then. I was just obeying those around me. I didn't understand anything about purpose. Purpose is the reason for you to be here, the something you have to do that will matter. Purpose is what gives your life meaning and significance. All I knew at seven years old about my purpose was that God was with me, and with God, all things were possible.

Before that day I sang because I was supposed to, because I didn't want to disappoint those around me—least of all God. I loved God with all of my seven-year-old heart. But that day, following both my love for God and my desire to please Sister Glenn and my family, I learned that I was born to sing. For the next three or so years at Mack Avenue Church of God in Christ "Fill My Cup" became my signature solo for the August convocation, and I cried every year I sang it. I'm certain that the congregation there thought I was crying because I was overwhelmed with the Holy Spirit. But I wasn't; I was afraid. But I learned even back then that it's possible to sing *through* your fear even if you can't sing away your fear.

~~ ~~

I loved the church, as did the rest of my sisters and brothers, not only because of the singing or friends, but also because we loved being surrounded by God's presence even though we didn't know it at the time. Anytime suited me just fine— Tuesday night, Wednesday night, Friday night, and all day Sunday were the times I looked forward to the most. I loved hands clapping, feet stamping, tambourines playing, and the beating of drums. But most of all I loved the sense of kinship and solidarity that existed among the membership, the way we greeted one another with a "holy" kiss and referred to one another as sisters and brothers. I felt safe at church. I felt wrapped in a cocoon of love and somebodyness whenever I walked through the doors and heard, "Hey, CeCe, meet me at the piano."

The words and rhythms of black church music filled me with such joy and sorrow, love and dread, longing and satisfaction, that I couldn't get enough of them, just as I couldn't get enough of God. I lived in constant fear as a child that perhaps I wasn't living up to my potential in God, that perhaps I wasn't good enough, loving enough, or kind enough. I wanted to please God so much that sometimes I bordered on the fanatic, or so my brothers claim. Once when I was a young girl I put myself on a fast. An ancient discipline of the church, fasting is a favorite among Pentecostals because it appeals to their fundamentalist teaching about sanctifying the body and mortifying the flesh for the sake of Christ. Besides its place as an important discipline to be exercised during Lent, the forty days between Ash Wednesday and Easter, and it is also undertaken to renew your commitment to the Christian journey. Our pastor, Elder Stacks, would call for the church members to join him in a fast for three to four days when he felt the need for the church to rally together around a spiritual cause. Being able to deny myself food—and sometimes even water—was my way to prove to God that I was willing to deny myself for God. It also proved to me that I was not as timid and afraid as I thought. I could be daring.

It was nothing strange for us as children to fast along with the adults. But this time I fasted alone. I made it for the first two days. By the third day, I felt myself becoming dizzy, too dizzy to stay on my feet. After a short time of playing outside, I had to take to my bed. I remember lying on my bed with my eyes closed, in a state of famished delirium, trying to take my nose off the smell of macaroni and cheese and sweet potatoes Mom was cooking in the kitchen. I wanted to see the fast through to the end, but my energy was draining. "God give me strength," I was praying inside. "Don't let me give up on this fast." Lying there contemplating my love for God and weighing my love for macaroni and cheese and sweet potatoes, all of a sudden I sensed a presence in my bedroom. Too weak and exhausted to open my eyes, I remained still. A voice whispered in my ear, "Rise, Lazaritha, rise." Before I could convince myself that an angel was visiting me, my brother Ronald's and my sister Angie's howling laughter brought me to my senses. "Girl, get up from there and eat. What's wrong with you?" They teased me for several days.

ЭС ЭЄ

As mature and precocious as circumstances and birth forced me to become, the truth is that deep inside I was always afraid as a child. I was afraid of the dark. I was afraid of strange noises. I was afraid of standing before crowds. I was afraid that something bad might happen to my parents. I was afraid to disobey God. I was afraid to say what was on my mind. One day, and I don't know when it happened, I stopped being afraid. I'm not exactly sure where all that fear went. All I know for certain is that one day I just sang through the fear. Much of it was a child's anxiety about the unknown—fears that all children experience more or less, at some time, when growing up. I have God to thank for not letting those fears get the best of me. I would never have achieved the things I've achieved if I'd remained chained by those fears.

The story of my life is, in many ways, the story of how God took one fear in particular, namely my fear of getting up in front of crowds, and used it to heal me of all my other fears. He did that by giving me a family and a gift that would not allow me to stay locked up inside myself. I am grateful for having been blessed with a family that saw to it that I had the venues for developing my musical talents. By surrounding me with a big, loving family, God made certain that I'd never be able to build a battalion of excuses for myself for always being afraid. I was born to sing.

A Rich Heritage

A rich heritage is part of me,
My people were uneducated but very smart you see.
They trusted in God, not in worldly strategies,
Believing in the power of prayer every step of the way
*   and seeing results consistently.*

The sick were healed,
The dead were raised,
I'm here today because of the prayers they prayed.

I could never repay them,
They gave me the benefits from the start.
I have little to do with what I have achievea,
I give credit and honor to those who were before, my rich
    heritage, the legacy given to me.

3

The Winans

❧ ❧

A good name is to be chosen rather than great riches,
loving favor rather than silver and gold.
—Prov. 22:1

I don't recall there being any
performing arts schools in Detroit back when I was growing
up. If there were any, my parents surely couldn't have afforded
to send me to them. The church was the only place in the black
community for kids like me to get our first chance at discovering our talents. We all heard the rhythms and studied the styles
of the great singers and choirs that lived in and visited Detroit,
and the youth choirs at my church were determined not to be
outdone. We kept up with the latest church song, and we knew
what we liked: we liked it fast and we liked it loud.

Although my parents favored the old-time quartet groups, mass choirs were the order of the day when I was growing up. Songs like Edwin Hawkins's "O Happy Day," which was recorded in 1969, had introduced a new sound in black church music. Our youth choirs sang at church services, musical conferences, and church convocations. Sometimes we were the best, and sometimes we were flat and bombed out. But what we learned about singing, about working together, and about striving to be excellent were lessons that stayed with each of us forever. Long before the Winans children branched out as performing artists basking in the limelight, we learned in the church how to work as a team, how to harmonize, how to provide backup to other singers, and how to pull our own weight. It was fun because we made it fun. The first sopranos showed off over the second sopranos, altos strutted their stuff over the sopranos, and tenors backed up the whole sound with their own smooth bravado. We learned how to deal with people. It wasn't until I got out and started singing outside my church that I began to imagine singing as something more than a hobby. At first it was just something I did with my family and friends at church. Once I began to see the power that music had over people—and once I saw the impact my singing had on people who didn't know me—I began to know that it was a gift from God.

Only the Lord knows where my parents came up with the money on their salaries to sponsor the family in concert every

year at Detroit's Mercy College in West Detroit. All I know
is that every year they found the money somehow and invited
all of Detroit out to join us in an evening of praising the Lord
in song. Christmas was traditionally the time for our concerts. Since it wasn't possible to buy gifts for all ten of their
children, my parents decided that rather than spend money
on toys that would be broken by February, they would put on
a holiday concert for gospel lovers in the city. The emphasis
of the concert every year was on love and family. Mom and
Dad were bent on reminding us all of the true spirit of
Christmas. "We may not be rich in things," my father might
say at the beginning of the concert, "but we are rich in love.
And that's what Christmas is all about." Then he would
quote Scripture:

> *"For God so loved the world that he gave his only*
> *begotten Son,*
> *that whosoever believeth in him*
> *should not perish, but have everlasting life."*

By singing as a family for the holiday season, the true
meaning of being blessed was driven home to us kids. The
Winans family annual holiday concerts reminded me once
again that being blessed was not about having things but
about having a heart to give love and to receive love. We
looked forward to our concert at the end of the year and spent

a lot of time planning it, which also had the added benefit of making us work together as a family. There was always so much to do to prepare for the concert: we had to learn how to pull off a concert on a meager budget. Things like finding music, rehearsing until the wee hours of the morning, renting sound equipment, running off programs, and buying or having Mom make inexpensive outfits kept us too busy to care about not exchanging material gifts at Christmas. It kept us too busy to bicker or to stay mad at one another. We had to cooperate in order to meet our goals. Sponsoring those concerts for us was the greatest gift Mom and Dad ever gave us. Those concerts gave us the experience we needed to be able to go off in our own directions later on and become the musicians and performers God intended us to be. From those concerts, we learned what it took to sing in public, what our strengths were as vocalists, and how to help compensate for one another's weaknesses. We learned to pull together and pool our resources. We learned the importance of relying upon one another. I will always be grateful to my parents for their precious gift of knowledge. Years later, the memory of what I learned from those concerts would serve me when it was time for BeBe and me to stand on the stage together and sing. And the memory of the Christmas concerts gave me strength when the time came for me to stand alone.

All of Detroit showed up for our family concerts, or so it seemed to my young eyes. The modest auditorium filled with seven hundred people felt like a stadium. I was past feeling terror at the thought of singing, but I still felt butterflies in my stomach whenever it was time to come onstage. With my family beside me, I could make it. Although the audience came primarily to hear my older brothers sing, who started out as the Testimonial Singers and then changed their name later to The Winans, nevertheless there was a respectable amount of applause for those of us who made up the lower half of the clan, referred to as the Winans Part II: Daniel, BeBe, Michael, and me. We didn't sing together a lot back then, only at our annual family concerts and on a few other special occasions throughout the city. But when we did sing together, our voices blended naturally and easily—we'd had so much practice singing together at home. Daniel has always had a beautiful, clear singing voice, and BeBe has always had a more outgoing and take-charge personality. He was the spokesperson for the younger group. My own voice, with its soft airy quality, brought a soft edge to our hymns and helped to infuse emotion and yearning to our music.

Eventually we started inviting various friends from the church's youth choir to join us to help lend more depth and dimension to our sound. Rita Henry was the first nonfamily member to join us. She had a great voice and stayed for a while. Then Marvie Wright joined. Marvie had a rich alto voice that had a wonderful texture to it. Colorful spunky Vicki Bowman, with her high soprano voice, brought much drama to our ensemble and could just plain sing like someone crazy. Vicki, who years later would marry my older brother Marvin, didn't mind taking the mike, strutting across the stage, and rearing back with all her might to bellow out a song. She kept the group in stitches with her hilarious sense of humor. Marvie, Vicki, and I were instant friends, and the two of them became like big sisters to me. When time came for me to lead my solo, with Winans Part II as my backup, Marvie and Vicki were my inspiration to sing better than I would have had they not been there. There is nothing like other women in the group to stir your singing feathers. One of the great things about growing up in the Pentecostal church is that everybody can sing—or so it seems—and that helped to keep us from ego tripping or becoming too boastful. If you won't get out there and sing, someone else will and can. But once you agree to get out there and sing, you'd better give it everything you had. Such a warm glow filled me deep within and swept throughout every part of my body when I sang my song, a radiance of power convincing me that it wasn't me but someone else singing through me. I sang for that radiance. Once I closed my eyes, it was like I became lost in the song, lost in a ray of light that kept beckoning me to step out, to trust the light, and to surrender to it.

Blessed assurance, Jesus is mine!
O what a foretaste of glory divine.
Heir of salvation, purchase of God.

Born of His Spirit, washed in His blood.
This is my story.
This is my song.
Praising my Savior All the day long.

❧ ❧

Winans Part II was its own sensation at the family concert, and from time to time we gave the Testimonial Singers a
run for their money. There was a happy and healthy amount
of competition going on between the younger singers in the
family and the older singers in the family. Just enough to keep
both groups on their toes. Just enough to keep us younger
ones hustling to learn more. "J-E-S-U-S," "Restoration,"
and "Break Up the Fallow Ground" by the Testimonial
Singers were audience favorites, and when my brothers sang
them during their part, everyone knew it was over. Their
contemporary sound and style appealed to the people in the
audience and made everyone go wild with joy. Back then
some of the songs we all sang were rearrangements of traditional church hymns, but most of the songs we sang were
originals written by my brother Marvin.

Dad was the master of ceremonies. He was always careful to emphasize to us and to the audience that this was no
show. "We're here to give God some praise for all of His
wonderful blessings to us. We want to let the world know
that being sanctified doesn't mean being solemn and sad.

With sanctification comes joy and happiness." By this point, he would be a little bit excited himself as he'd throw his hands up in the air and give a wave offering to the Lord. He reminded everyone that we weren't there at Mercy College playing church or trying to mimic the ways of the world. His children's singing was a ministry, a beacon of light, to someone, especially to some young person, who was lost and about to give up. The Winans family concerts were a favorite among the young and old back then in Detroit, but especially among the young. Dad's jovial, talkative manner made him well-suited for introducing and transitioning from one performance to the next. "No one else but me has enough children to fill up a whole two-hour concert, and so, ladies and gentlemen, please put your hands together for this next set of my children who are as dear to me as Angie, Debbie, and my daughter-in-law Regina, the youngsters who've just finished their number. Come on and give Winans Part II a hand as they come on. Praise the Lord."

Dad always had a heart for the young, perhaps because he was still young himself. What he and Mom lost in marrying so young, they found in having ten children within seventeen years between the eldest child and the youngest child. We kept them young, or so we tried, with our youthful antics, our interests, and our contemporary songs.

We were deeply influenced by the new sounds, coming especially from the West Coast, by young recording artists, especially artists like Andrae Crouch, son of a bishop, and the Edwin Hawkins Family, both products like ourselves of the rich and jubilant rhythms of the Church of God in Christ church (C.O.G.I.C.). Crouch's "Through It All" and the Hawkins' family's "O Happy Day" introduced a new sound to gospel music that appealed to young people like ourselves. Their combination of lively rhythms and uplifting lyrics made them an instant hit. The fact that both Andrae Crouch and Edwin Hawkins teamed up with members of their family to make their music was not lost on us. We had the C.O.G.I.C. church to thank for our music, despite its severe restrictions on our social lives. Music was the one area where as young people we were allowed to spread our wings and to push the boundaries. This was thanks to musicians like Mrs. Mattie Moss Clark, who was the director of music for the Southwest Michigan Choir and then became president and director of the music department for the entire C.O.G.I.C. denomination.

New sounds were popping up in church choir lofts across the country. Young singers flocked to hear Mrs. Clark's music and to watch her dramatic orchestrations. She believed in perfection and giving God your best. Of course, I wasn't permitted to go out late at night and attend her famous "Midnight Musicals" at the denominational conventions, but I felt their influence as my brothers regaled us with stories and reenactments of the sights and sounds of up-and-coming gospel talent from across the country: the Hawkins singers, Donald Vails, the gospel saxophonist Vernard Johnson, Andrae and Sandra Crouch, the Clark sisters (Mattie Moss Clark's daughters), to name a few. My favorite was Tramaine Hawkins, wife of Walter Hawkins and lead singer in many of the Hawkinses' songs. Her graceful singing, coupled with her willowy dark beauty, became my inspiration for a sound of elegant praise to the Lord.

Singing kept our family together and helped us spend more time together than most families. As the older boys started growing up, taking jobs, moving out of the house, and starting families of their own, the house on Woodingham remained the hub for the early years of my brothers' rehearsals and all our family consultations. Mom and Grandmother Howze's cooking and Dad's sage advice kept everyone in touch. Dad managed my brothers in the early days of their careers and had always taken an active part in raising his children. He was proud of the fact that he had a close relationship with his sons and was careful to stay on top of their career plans, determined that their growing popularity never go to their heads or make them lose sight of the responsibility that comes with blessing. Borrowing from Jesus' words, Dad admonished them, "What does it profit you to gain the whole world and lose your soul?" Then he'd quickly add a little proverb of his own: "If you get proud and lifted up, then you'll go down like the *Titanic.*"

Singing together as a family also gave us a way to witness as a family to other families. We modeled for them that it was possible to stay together. With love and forgiveness it was possible to heal and to stay together. We rarely spoke openly and publicly about the disagreements and fallings-out we had at home, but there were some. There's no way in a family of twelve that we did not have our feelings hurt, our hearts broken, our needs unmet. But as a family we survived it.

Music allowed us to spread the gospel to a broader audience than we otherwise might have been able to reach. Through music the Spirit wooed, convicted, saved, and set people free, and to think that my voice was one of the instruments for doing this was humbling. Singing was a ministry, a calling, a gift from God, with a way of touching the least likely people. Even those who'd never paid attention to gospel music or associated it with their parents' old-time ways, even those who hadn't stepped inside a church door in years since moving out of their parents' house—they were moved by our music. And those still living in their parents' house who hated going to church, found it boring, or wouldn't be caught dead in a church choir were even more swept up by our concerts. "If we had singing like this at our church," someone would come up to one of us afterward and say, "I'd join and would never leave the church." It was the combination of seeing how young we were—Angie and Debbie at no more than eleven and nine, Michael, Daniel,

BeBe, and me at twenty-one, nineteen, sixteen, and fourteen, and the top half, the Winans, all in their twenties—and hearing us sing with such confidence and passion that brought many out to hear us. Those who knew what we were singing about—who, like us, were good and faithful members of their local churches, members of their own local youth choir, fellow pilgrims along the "saved, sanctified, and filled with the Holy Ghost" journey—clapped, stomped, and cheered us on, knowing that this was about as much "entertainment" as Scripture and their parents would allow.

The Winans

We're gifted to sing songs of praise,
Committed to God for the rest of our days.
Chosen to spread a little heaven on earth,
All year long we celebrate Christ's birth.

We're a close-knit family,
But at times it seems we are far apart.
Guilty of hurting each other's feelings,
Afterwards forgiving from the heart.

Raised in holiness in the Church of God in Christ,
We received our training to live a Christian life.
We loved to laugh, tease, and make fun,
Our parents taught us to love everyone.

We're sinners saved by grace,
Even though we are saints, we make mistakes.
If we fall we get back up, we must finish the race.
For our life's reward is to see Jesus face-to-face.

Saving the lost, encouraging the discouraged, healing the broken heart, restoring families—this has always been the message of the music that nursed me as a child. It was the message of the music in my church, the message I heard at home, and it's been the message I've tried to pass along in my music. I have seen music change people's lives, and I know from my own life the tremendous effect it can have on young people. Through our family concerts at Mercy College there in Detroit I saw young people responding to positive, uplifting messages of hope, love, joy, and holiness through their smiles, tears, outstretched hands, and the expressions of joy on their faces. Those memories have stayed with me throughout my career as a performer. They are what I draw on in the occasional moments when in my dressing room, after a performance, I catch myself wondering about my journey. I think of our family concerts at Mercy College, and I know that through my grandfather's determination to bless my family with his name, my father's willingness to forgive, and my parents' sacrifices to keep music and the Lord in my heart—through it all, God was preparing me for my future.

4

Lessons

A wise man will hear and increase learning,
and a man of understanding will attain wise counsel.
—*Prov. 1:5*

*T*here is a difference between being able to sing and becoming a singer. I knew for the longest time that I had a gift from God to sing, but still I couldn't bring myself to dream of actually becoming a singer.

How does a girl from Detroit with a talent for singing *not* dream of becoming a professional singer? Detroit provided little black girls with role models of black success. Growing up in the same city that produced soulful divas such as Diana Ross and Aretha Franklin would make it easy for any girl to imagine herself as a singer—or so you would think. But dreams are about the heart, not about geography. A confident girl from Sparta, Georgia, or Freeman, Ohio, or Tyler, Texas, stood a better chance than I did of making her dream of singing come true. I lacked the confidence. I couldn't imagine myself as a singer, and I didn't believe I had what it took.

One girl's dream is another girl's fantasy. Aspiring for a regular, nice, respectable, nine-to-five job was my safe dream. Setting my hopes on becoming a singer was a fantasy I didn't dare dwell on. Singing was about family and God, not about money or being out front. No matter how many times people complimented me for my singing, I never imagined a full blown career in music for myself. It was God using me, God singing through me. Everyone I knew who sang as a ministry also had a day job. You squeezed your ministry into whatever time or energy was left *after* you finished your day job, just as my parents had done. I was determined to get a nice paying job after school, and I too would fit singing into whatever energies and time were left over.

At what age do girls start putting a cap on their dreams? Experts say it's around twelve, thirteen, and fourteen. That's right about the time I began asking myself whether I could really sing, whether I was pretty enough, whether I was graceful enough and tall enough. But the truth is I just didn't believe in myself. Becoming a professional singer required guts and a whole lot of self-esteem, which I didn't have. To believe that I, CeCe Winans, had what it took to be a singer smacked of egotism, and I only wanted so much to please God. I didn't know how to believe in God and myself at the same time. I didn't know that the two could go hand in hand. My faith helped me carry on with the daily challenges of life, but I didn't know how to draw on that faith to make me soar.

According to the religiously conservative background in which I grew up, boys are the ones who are expected to be leaders and should be the ones standing in the spotlight. It came as no surprise to anyone in the family when in the 1970s my four older brothers started singing and performing professionally. The Testimonial Singers had changed their name by the early 1980s to The Winans. Ronald, Marvin, Carvin, and now Michael were an immediate hit. Pretty soon invitations poured in from throughout Detroit and beyond for my brothers to sing at various concerts. All those years of singing around the family piano, singing in the backseat of the car to and from school, singing in the Sunshine Band at Mack Avenue and in the youth choirs, in state and district choirs, were paying off.

The whole family was bursting at the seams with pride over my brothers' accomplishments. As their adoring little sister, I was so proud. So many times I had sat around the piano as a little girl listening to them work out the right chords for each of their parts. Now The Winans were making a name for themselves and for the entire family. I admired them for their courage and their hard work. They were doing what they were meant to do: stand before large audiences of people singing songs of inspiration and hope. It was when they met and paired up with California gospel legend Andrae Crouch, another child of the Pentecostal church, that their careers began to take off. When they landed their first recording contract in 1981 with Light records and called back home with the news, everybody in the family squealed and shouted and praised God. Mom and Dad wept tears of joy. God had upheld my grandfather's prophecy that our family would spread God's word through song. God had also blessed my mother and father's efforts to keep us together as a family and close to God through music. When the time came for my brothers to record their first album Dad accompanied my brothers to Los Angeles, and Mom followed later. My parents wanted to be with my brothers, and my brothers wanted my parents there as well.

But even with my brothers' example, it still didn't dawn on me that the same was possible for me. Singing, recording albums, and traveling around the world spreading God's word through music were things I still dared not dream for myself. I was content to retreat into the background, out of the spotlight, where good, modest Pentecostal girls like myself were expected to dream and live out their existence. It was enough to be able to sing at church. It was challenging enough just singing lead in the choir. But now I had learned how to surrender myself to a song. I'd close my eyes, open my mouth, and let the song take me and an audience where it wanted us to go.

Besides singing, typing was the next thing I was good at. It sounds funny now, but during my teenage years I thought about becoming a court stenographer. Miss Guidon, the guidance counselor at Mumford High, was always very encouraging to me. Whenever I had a down day, I would fall into her office and say, "I don't know if I can make it." She was always encouraging, yet firm. "You're such a talented young girl, Priscilla. You can be whatever you want to be." I liked the way "court stenographer" sounded. Never mind that I'd never been in a courtroom a day in my life. Never mind that I didn't know a soul who was a court stenographer. My ignorance only lent it an air of mystery and gravity. Compared to the many career options available to young girls these days, aspiring to be a court stenographer may not sound particularly grand. But for a little girl from Detroit who had never ventured too far from her Pentecostal, close-knit family, becoming a court stenographer was a stretch of the soul, a profession, a good, steady job, and a way out of poverty. That was my only requirement. I was determined not to be stuck in poverty. As an officer of the court, I felt that my future would be secure, I reasoned. Girls now are encouraged to aspire to become judges or lawyers, but that would mean I would have to be out front, talking in the spotlight. As a court stenographer I'd get to sit in the background, with my eyes cast down, steadily transcribing and taking in the sights and sounds of other people's drama, feeling their sorrow, narrating their pain, absorbing their points of view, and best of all, listening in on their fates. I hadn't yet learned to let the light of my soul shine forth.

I didn't have a lot of friends at Mumford High. My conservative upbringing kept me from hanging out with a lot of people. It wasn't just my longer-than-usual skirts and dresses, I'm sure. I was a city girl who didn't wear makeup or nail polish, who never wore the flashy earrings that were the rage at the time, and who didn't wear revealing blouses. (Pentecostal boys weren't so easily recognized in a crowd because no restrictions were placed on how they dressed.) Movies were out, and parties were forbidden by my folks. I was different. The few invitations I got to join sleep-overs, I had to bow out with excuses. "Sorry, but I've got to stay home and baby-sit my younger sisters." I never even brought up the invitations to my parents. I knew their answer.

"Do you all do anything other than go to church?" one girl at school asked me.

"Of course," I shot back. "We go to the park, the bowling alley, the skating rink."

"You do?" she said, looking surprised.

"Sure, our church sponsors outings like these for young people all the time," I said proudly.

"Oh," she responded, shaking her head.

Because I rarely had anything hip or intelligent to add to the conversations around the lockers or those that took place in the girls' gym class, I was simply a loner. I tried not to care, and for the most part, I didn't. But sometimes I found myself wondering what it would feel like to be popular.

Singing in the school choir at Mumford High and singing in the youth choir at Shalom Temple, where we were now members, kept me busy and occupied throughout much of my high school. My upbringing continued to define the kind of music I was allowed to sing. The repertoire for the high school choir consisted of old spirituals and religious and inspirational lyrics, which convinced Mom and Dad to let me sing. Besides, I needed the music credit to graduate. Singing in the school choir was the only place where I was not just different—I was special. There the special quality of my alto voice meant that I was frequently chosen to sing special parts. I came as close as I ever would to being popular, to being one of the gang, and to being accepted because being able to sing gave me an edge in the competitive social world of adolescents. Even though I was a Holy Roller, everyone knew that I could sing, and so I had a certain amount of status.

Being Skip Winans's daughter meant that courting boys was not an option. Besides, I was much too shy for that. I never lacked male admirers, however, even though I stayed pretty much to myself and spent what extra time I had studying or singing. A few intrepid souls tried to strike up conversations at the school locker or tried passing me notes in class: "Will you go with me?" one of them might ask. "Go with you where?" I replied. I didn't have a clue. A few boys caught my eye, but it never amounted to very much. The truth is that I was scared. Boys meant trouble. One kiss and I was certain I would get pregnant. I was determined not to wind up with ten children like my mother. Ten kisses would lead to ten children, I reasoned. Keeping to myself was my way of protecting myself from the things I didn't understand. As for the few really intrepid would-be suitors who did try to ask me out, take my hand, or walk me home, by the end of the semester they usually discovered that Priscilla Winans didn't have just one, three, five, but seven brothers, each one crazier and bulkier than the other. So I was usually left to walk home alone and unescorted from school. Having seven brothers was like having seven fathers. They were handy to have around if you ever got in trouble and needed protection, but they could be a nuisance if you were lonely and wanted someone to talk to.

In fact, my brothers could be ruthless on any would-be suitors of any of their sisters. One day, I told myself, I would find someone who loved me enough to stand up to my brothers' harassments and their mock threats. Until then I would have to content myself with occasional flings, casual conversations at the locker between classes, light-hearted teasing and flirtation at choir meetings, stolen glances at youth meeting, and snatches of conversation on the telephone. The truth is that I had my share of the secret crushes on popular boys in the school and at church, boys who probably wouldn't have given me the time of day if they knew they were a part of my daydreams, but I was much too plain and simple to catch anyone's eyes, or so I told myself. One day when I grew up, I would shed my plain and simple exterior and boys would look at me and see that I was . . . well, lovely. That's what I wanted to be: lovely. The day might never come when anyone would think of me as beautiful, but there was a chance that I might be considered lovely.

I longed for that glow of calm, self-assurance, and confidence that flowed from the inside that turns a plain woman into a lovely creature.

Church is where I was surrounded by friends and comrades who had similar interests and values. By the time I entered high school the family had joined a new church, Shalom Temple, a nondenominational Pentecostal church in West Detroit. Not only did I sing in the young people's choir, along with the rest of my sisters and brother, but I also took turns with BeBe directing many of the songs the choir sang. After a while some of the choir members in the back of the choir stand complained that they couldn't see my small hands from where they stood. My hands, they complained, were just too small to see over all the heads, and no one could make out what as director, from one moment to the next, I was instructing the choir to do. "Lift your hands higher, CeCe," someone would invariably yell from the back when I stood to direct. Most of the jabs came from family members, who teased me mercilessly about everything from my hairstyle to the expressions on my face. Despite my efforts to direct as I'd seen some of my brothers do, by the end of the song my discomfort must have shown on my face, and the choir collapsed with laughter. So would I. I didn't mind their good-natured razzing. We were family. They were all pariahs at school like me and needed a place to belong. When we were together at church, we reminded ourselves that despite what students at school thought about us, we were normal teenagers, blessed with and guilty of all the traits associated with being a teenager: we laughed when we were supposed to be serious. We fought even while loving one another, we goofed off when we were supposed to pay attention, and we tipped off to the store to buy candy when as girls we should have been in "purity classes," learning how to sit with our knees together and our skirts down. The boys were supposed to be in their own "purity classes" somewhere in another part of the building, learning how to stand without slumping and how to keep their hands off the girls. In other words, we were normal teenagers who shared secrets with and complained about our parents to one another. Away from the watchful eyes of our strict parents, of course. But above all, we worshiped God together, mostly through song.

Some of us were Holy Rollers in the literal sense of the

word. When the spirit was high, one of us could be found speaking in tongues or stretched out in the spirit on the floor. Mostly, we shouted, clapped, stomped, rocked, and did everything short of break-dance before God. Choir singing was our delight because it was the one place in the church where we enjoyed an element of independence. The adults permitted us, for the most part, to do what we pleased in the choir: we chose what music we wanted to sing. They helped raise money for new choir robes and permitted us drums, guitars, and organs, which we used to pump up the beat. As we matured, the lessons we learned from singing matured. We learned how to sing four-part harmony, how to blend our voices without losing our own special timbre, how to appreciate the talents of a good accompanist because of his or her ability to help you pace yourself. Best of all, we learned the creative, artistic, and heartfelt aspects of singing: if you don't feel what you're singing, neither will your audience; always give your best whether you're singing to a "packed house" or to a "slack house." We were satisfied, at least most of us were, with the strict, seemingly old-fashioned customs our parents passed along to us, filled as we were with both gratitude for and fear of the adults in our lives. There's an unacknowledged appreciation that you have parents who love you enough to have expectations of you, and then there's a grudging fear that borders on resentment of the power they ultimately have over you. At the heart of our parents' harsh ways was their nagging fear for the lives of their young black teenage children being raised on the streets of Detroit, but that fear would not dawn on us until years later, when our time came to raise children and to choose some blueprint for the task.

❧ ❧

By my classmates' standards I was square, and in my siblings' eyes I was spoiled.

"CeCe is the favorite," Angie and Debbie complained.

"CeCe never gets a whipping," Daniel and BeBe would protest. No one bothered to notice that a butt whipping is not the only way to learn. Some of life's most painful floggings are dealt without anyone lifting a hand. Shame at betraying a loved one's trust has its own sting.

Marvie Wright and I came up with a plan for getting to the Northwest Activity Center for a gospel concert. Marvie and I worked together at Coney Island Hot Dog at the local mall, and both of us loved good singing. We had to work too late to catch a ride with my brothers or any of the other young people from church, and so we had to come up with our own transportation. The problem was that neither of us drove. I was about fifteen, and Marvie was sixteen. We were determined to go to the gospel concert, and we came up with a plan. Actually, Marvie came up with a plan. I repeat, Marvie came up with a plan.

"Your father doesn't know that I can't drive," she said.

"What's your point?' I asked.

"Let's let him think that I have my license and ask him for the car." Marvie had an ID card that looked just like a driver's license, picture and all.

"Are you out of your mind?"

"Do you want to go or not?" I agreed, but I was convinced it wouldn't work. I knew my father would turn us down flat.

"My car?" my father asked. "Are you girls crazy?"

"Please, Daddy, we'll drive carefully."

"Marvie, you must have your license, 'cause I know CeCe doesn't have hers."

I gulped.

"Yes, sir, I can drive." Marvie answered so quickly and confidently I had to stare at her. She showed him the fake ID and didn't flinch. Neither did she lie. Not really. He asked about a license, and she assured him that she could drive. The difference was enough to keep us out of hell for lying—or so we thought, not realizing that misleading someone is just as bad as outright lying to the person.

Dad knew how much we wanted to go. It wasn't like it was a Jackson 5 concert. It was a gospel concert. He knew my brothers were sure to be somewhere in the auditorium to check up on me. He looked carefully at both of us before answering. Marvie looked back at him intently, never blinking an eye, with just enough poise and pleading in her eyes to seem trustworthy. I kept my eyes on Marvie, lest Dad detect my nervousness. I was scared he would see the hesitation in my eyes and know something in our story was amiss.

"Be careful," Dad said, reaching in his pockets and handing Marvie the keys.

It was too good to believe. Who would have thought? Dad never let me out of his sight. He never let any of us girls go anywhere without one of our brothers tagging along. That would be the first of two times that my father answered yes to my request to be allowed to go somewhere new and different. The other would be a few years later when I had a chance to start a whole new life in Charlotte, North Carolina, singing on a Christian broadcast.

Shame and exhilaration washed over me. Marvie and I looked at each other—neither of us thought that my father would fall for our story, but he did. He *trusted* us. He knew Marvie's people were good sanctified people, that her father, Elder Wright, was the pastor of Miller Memorial Church of God in Christ. I was his baby girl, who'd never given him much trouble. What was there not to trust this once? It was too late to turn back. The keys were in our hands. We were afraid to go, but we were also too ashamed to tell Dad the truth.

"Lord have mercy on our souls," I mumbled to myself as Marvie started up the car. Marvie had never driven on an expressway before—she had only been allowed a few spins around Kmart parking lots with one of her brothers. With me on the passenger side alternating between begging Jesus for mercy and giving her what few street directions I could remember, Marvie drove Dad's car, cautiously and slowly down what felt like every side street in Detroit, her knuckles gripping the steering wheel in terror. Every policeman in Detroit was on the street that night, it seemed. I was a wreck, and so was Marvie. Between Jesus and Marvie, my father's car managed to stay in the middle of the road and get to where we were going.

No sooner had we arrived but we were busted. Both Marvie's brothers and my brothers met us in the auditorium. They were shocked to see us. "How did you girls get here?" "We drove," Marvie answered nonchalantly. I knew she'd lost her mind—this was no time to tell the truth. "Drove? What nut let you drive his car?" one of them asked. They knew that Marvie did not have a license. When we told them we had Dad's car, everyone nearly passed out. "Are you two crazy?" Daniel yelled, turning to look at me. "Daddy said it was all right," I said, knowing it was a lame comment as soon as I said it. Daniel snatched the keys out of Marvie's hand, and after calling home to tell both sets of parents, drove us home.

Finally, Miss Goody-Goody was going to get it.

I think I would have preferred my father to have yelled, or screamed, but he didn't. I would have understood if he had taken a strap to me or grounded me for the rest of my life, but he did none of these things. He neither yelled nor stormed about the house. He didn't even lift a finger. He just stood in the doorway to my bedroom and looked at me hard and long. The look of disappointment on his face as I told him the whole story made me want to run and hide in shame. I had lied to him. I hadn't told a lie, but I had lied just the same.

It seemed like an eternity. Dad didn't speak. I kept expecting him to ask "Why?" But he didn't. If he had asked "Why did you lie?" or "Why did you betray my trust?" I wouldn't have had anything intelligent to say. Marvie and I had driven my Dad's car without so much as a scratch to ourselves or to Dad's car. But the harm done to my father's trust in his oldest girl seemed irrecoverable.

Dad didn't say anything—he simply shook his head. Part of what he must have felt was embarrassment that he had been suckered by two teenagers. My father is a strong man, and he's also smart and wise, much too smart and wise to be fooled by his children. Or so he had thought.

My brothers were probably disappointed that Dad didn't beat me, but my father *is* smart and wise. He didn't have to beat me because he knew that I would beat up on myself. The first lesson I learned from that experience is that the heart dispenses its own retribution. My father didn't have to punish me. My love for him saw to it that the shame for what I had done gave me a better flogging than any strap could have done. If my dad had whipped me, when it was over I would have been done with the pain. But the shame I felt took a long time to run its course. I felt horrible going to church the next morning, knowing that I had sinned against my father, dishonored him and shamed him. It made me want to cry for days. I loved my mother and father, and when you love someone you care what that person thinks about you.

Dad could have shunned me or made me walk around in shame for weeks until he was satisfied that I had been humiliated enough, but he didn't. He isn't that kind of man. I had disappointed a wonderful man, but Skippy Winans was more than a proud man, he was also a father who loved his daughter and was willing to forgive her. My father taught me the second lesson. I learned from that incident one of the most valuable lessons I have ever learned: my father taught me what it means to forgive someone you love.

Lessons

There's a lesson to be learned in everything you see,
Whether it's in watching a bird flying or surveying a
*   beautiful palm tree.*

The Creator of this world is the One who holds the key,
Kneeling at His feet is where we should be.

To find all of life's answers, the puzzle's missing piece,
So many lessons to be learned, some more important
*   than the rest,*
But learning to trust and obey God is by far the best.

5

Path of Opportunity

The steps of a good man are ordered by the Lord,
and He delights in his way.
—Psalms 37:23

Once in a while something happens, an opportunity comes along, a phone call, a knock at the door, that is so unexpected, so out of the ordinary, so unimaginable, so unplanned that you know it must have been dispatched from wherever it is that miracles come. You run it through your mind a thousand times, trying to track it down, wondering how your name came up, wondering who did you know who you didn't know that you knew, looking for some sign you could have caught but didn't because you weren't paying attention, something you missed but now didn't know it, determined to find the formula for anticipating a miracle. But you're stumped. You can't track a miracle. You never saw it coming. And that's fine. Because if you had seen it coming, then it wouldn't have been such a miracle.

The year 1981 would prove to be a very pivotal year in my life, forcing me out and into the world, launching me on a path I hadn't foreseen, presenting me with new challenges and new opportunities. For every new challenge and opportunity that presented itself to me, however, there was one condition: I had to surrender all the comfort and security I had grown to rely upon.

One day we got a call from a friend of our family Howard McCrary, a musical director for the *PTL Show*, a religious broadcast based in North Carolina, inviting BeBe and me to come down and audition for some openings they had. I knew I was on the verge of becoming something, but I didn't have a clue as to what. All I knew was that I didn't want to be a court stenographer any longer. The family knew and trusted Howard McCrary because he'd been a friend for years. He'd worked with my brothers on some of their recordings, and he was a friend of Andrae Crouch. Howard was hoping to recruit new black talent to infuse the television show with more soul, and he thought BeBe and I would fit in well with the group.

Now I had just graduated from high school and started studying cosmetology. I'd delayed studying to be a court stenographer, thinking that I would train to be a cosmetologist first to make some money. I knew I was good at fixing and styling hair. I had to be. My mom had burned my ears so many times with the hot iron that I had started doing my own hair to protect myself! I wanted to go to beauty school first and then proceed to college because my parents didn't have the money to send me. I stayed at home, thinking I could save some money, enroll in cosmetology school, and set about getting my license. Styling hair was something I enjoyed, and it allowed me to be creative. I knew firsthand how crazy black women were about their hair. Our hair remains our number one possible source of self-transformation for us. It's the one thing we can control.

But this phone call from North Carolina came out of the blue for me, for BeBe, and for the family. Just thinking about it sent shivers down my spine. Someone actually thought I sang well enough to invite me to come to North Carolina. I knew next to nothing about North Carolina except for the fact that it was in the South, and all I knew about the South were the stories of civil rights protests that had taken place there in the 1960s. North Carolina didn't seem to be one of the states that came to mind when I thought about police dogs, racist governors, Ku Klux Klan marches, church bombings, and the murders of civil rights activists. It was only years later that I found out that in fact North Carolina was the site of one of the first student sit-ins, when four black students from North Carolina

Agricultural and Technical State University marched into the Woolworth's in Greensboro, North Carolina, sat down at its lunch counter, and refused to leave until they were served.

North Carolina may as well have been an exotic island for a girl who'd only been to school, to church, to camp, and to a few family outings around the state. I wasn't sure I wanted to uproot and leave my family for even a strange exotic island in the South, but I was very impressed with the fact that I had it to consider as an option. The real miracle would be getting my father to agree to let me go.

Neither BeBe nor I had heard of the *PTL Show,* a Christian family television program that was broadcast outside of Charlotte, North Carolina. That it boasted millions of viewers from across the world was news to both of us. No one in the family had ever heard of Jim or Tammy Faye Bakker. My exposure to white Christians was virtually nonexistent back then. The reasons for this are obvious I suppose, and it's sad. We all serve the same God, and we should all make an effort to come together for worship.

I can't speak for BeBe, but I can say that if I had known of *PTL*'s immense fame and popularity as a Christian broadcasting satellite I probably would not have found the nerve to go out and audition for it. At the time I thought it was some local, at most regional, television program that Christians from as far away as Detroit could pick up maybe if they had good antennas. Sometimes what you don't know is good for you. It allows you to take advantage of opportunities and things you might not have had you known better.

BeBe was ready to jump at the chance to pursue music full time. He kept his hands in anything that had anything to do with music. He was always writing songs. When our big break came along, BeBe was *ready*.

"I don't know, BeBe," I said, always slow to try something new. It would be our pattern for years to come: BeBe aggressive and impulsive, me apprehensive and cautious. Besides, I was already enrolled in cosmetology school. "We don't know these people," I said.

"What's there to know?" he asked. "Howard is out there, and we know Howard."

"But what if we get out there and find out it's all a hoax?"

He looked at me as if I were crazy. "Then we come back home."

"Aren't you the least bit scared?" I asked, knowing the answer already. "Besides, what makes you think Dad is going to let us go?" Now that made him flinch.

BeBe was nineteen years old and a man. He knew Dad wouldn't prevent him from going. He knew he would be following in the footsteps of our older brothers, The Winans, who had recorded their first album a year earlier. But I was a girl. Neither of us could imagine Dad agreeing to let me go all the way across the country to Charlotte. The only place that I had ever gone to stay overnight was to Grandmother

Howze's house. Requesting to go to North Carolina was not the kind of test I had in mind.

I knew how much of a mama's boy BeBe was. I thought he might have second thoughts, but I was wrong. He was eager and excited. What others see as an obstacle, BeBe sees as a challenge. The thought of packing and moving across the country never frightened him. He loved adventure.

"I don't know BeBe," I said, "I can't see Dad going for it."

"Let's talk to Mom first," he suggested. "If she agrees, we know we're halfway there."

Mom was excited about us going, but her response was, "Ask your father." She knew instinctively that it was a great opportunity, and she had warned Dad to keep an open mind to something BeBe and CeCe wanted to ask him. She knew how excited both of us were about the possibility. She also knew how scared I was to get my hopes up.

I was curious. Very curious. I was also honored. At the same time, I felt apprehensive. It had never dawned on me to leave everything and everyone I knew and loved and move away. I'd thought about moving out of Mom and Dad's house and was looking forward to saving enough money to get my own apartment. But leaving Detroit, my family, my church, and everything familiar was another thought.

Dad didn't take long to make up his mind. "You can go as long as the two of you go together." BeBe and I were shocked. He had responded so quickly that it was almost scary. When Mom told him about our request, Dad had already prayed about it. We had satisfied all his questions about where we were going, what we'd be doing, where we would stay, and how we were going.

"You mean CeCe can go too?" my brother said, speaking up when he saw I was too stunned to speak.

"As long as you promise to take care of your sister and look out for her," Dad said, sitting back down.

This was the second time my father had said yes to my request to go in my own direction. His renewed trust moved me greatly, first because he had cause to mistrust me after the incident with the car. But also everybody knew how protective my father was of his girls, especially "Sister," his oldest girl. He couldn't bear the thought of anyone or anything hurting his little girl. But he also wanted what was best for me.

Memories of singing with the Lemon Gospel Chorus probably helped to make him understand what an opportunity this invitation was for BeBe and me. My parents never tired of talking about the joys, the freedom, the sense of purpose and direction they found in singing with other young people, and they couldn't allow themselves to deny those same experiences to their own children. Singing for the Lord in the Lemon Gospel Chorus was their reference point for imagining the experiences that awaited us. They were always happy when opportunities arose for the Winans children to live out their parents' earliest secret ambitions. It's as if one generation opens themselves up for the dream so that it can take root and come to life in the following generation.

When I heard my father say that I could go to North Carolina with BeBe to audition for the *PTL Show* I stopped holding my breath and started breathing. Then I squealed. Then I hollered. It was another miracle, another sign from God. BeBe and I both jumped up and down, screaming for joy.

I was determined to let neither God nor my father down this time.

❧ ❧

It was my first time away from home on my own, and I didn't know what to expect. What kind of people would I meet out in North Carolina? I didn't know. I had no idea. I needed the Lord to direct my path. We had been taught at home to love everybody. Would I be accepted? What if I got there and found out I couldn't sing after all? What if I weren't the kind of singer they are looking for? What if I didn't belong? How would I face everyone back home if I had to return? A month or two after Howard McCrary had called, I sat on the plane paralyzed with doubts. "This is a fine time to run scared," I thought to myself, "some thirty thousand miles up in the sky."

I didn't want to be off to North Carolina to chase after some glory for myself. I wanted to go home. I'd seen all the hard work my older brothers had put into their work: singing

and traveling, even for Jesus, can be heartbreaking work—
broken promises, bad deals, endless rehearsals, last-minute
changes, a sore, aching throat, and strained relationships. I
didn't want any part of that. All I wanted to do was sing for
Jesus. If the Lord was in fact beckoning me to come out to
North Carolina to sing for Him, I was prepared to give up
everything I had planned for myself to do what God wanted.

My motives for going one thousand miles across the
country were not purely religious and altruistic, however. A
side of me was curious to see if I could do it. I wanted to see
how far the gift God had given me would take me. I still
didn't think of myself as a singer. I could sing, and I thought
of myself as just someone who was on her way out to North
Carolina to sing Christian music on television with other
singers. But I wasn't a singer. *Singer* meant women like
Mahalia Jackson, Nancy Wilson, Barbra Streisand, and
Dionne Warwick, women who had shaped their careers by
singing alone onstage. I didn't want to be alone, and I didn't
know how to be alone. To call myself a singer would mean I
would have to be alone, independent, and onstage in front of
thousands of people, pulling a whole show off alone. Not
counting the solos at church and at the family's annual concerts, I had never sung alone. There were always members of
my family by my side whenever I sang. My family all sang
inspirational music for the Lord, some of us were more well
known and successful than others, but we sang as a family.

None of us had ever thought anything about branching out alone, on solo careers. That was not part of our world. Families singing together was an honored tradition in the Pentecostal church, with a long list of black gospel music families that sang together: the Staple Singers, the Hawkins Singers, the O'Neal Twins, Clara Ward and the Ward Singers, Andrae and Sandra Crouch. Singing is what bound our family together, and that was the way I wanted it to be as BeBe and I made our way out to North Carolina in the fall of 1981.

I imagined that whatever future awaited us, it awaited us together as sister and brother. It was a miracle that we were going, a miracle that we'd been asked to try out for a spot, a miracle from God that defied explanation.

The Right Path
There are many roads,
but only one for you:
Acknowledge the Lord in all your ways
and He will carry you through.

Life's journey is full of surprises,
both good and bad.
Let God lead your every step
and you will find the perfect path.

The path of opportunity
that will take you to your destiny,
in order to hear it when it knocks
you must listen very closely.

Time and chance happens to us all
so recognize when it's your turn
to walk by faith and totally
trust, never wavering but standing firm.

6

Over the Rainbow

We do not know what to do,
but our eyes are upon you, O God.
—*2 Chron. 20:12*

*L*ike Dorothy in the movie *The Wizard of Oz* taking one glance at that yellow brick road, knowing that she and her terrier, Toto, weren't in Kansas anymore, BeBe and I took one look at the grounds at *PTL* and knew we weren't in Detroit anymore. We looked at each other with wonder. We'd never seen so many trees and open spaces in our lives. We certainly didn't know that people could live so well and comfortably.

"Where are we?" BeBe asked, looking around in amazement.

"Boy, shut up," I shot back in a whisper. "Don't let people know you've never been anywhere." But he was right, we hadn't been anywhere like this.

The grounds of Heritage USA, the name of the campgrounds where *PTL* ministries were broadcast, were lavish and strikingly well kept. It was like something out of an airline travel magazine. The broad expansive buildings, the pools and the lakes, the lawns, and the parks were a sight to behold for kids born and raised in a northern urban sprawl. We were too cool to gawk and point, but we were not above letting our mouths drop. The Heritage Grand Hotel on Main Street was large enough to lodge some five hundred people and was filled with beautiful restaurants and shops. Over in the distance was the Heritage Village Church, where nightly camp meetings and Sunday worship took place. The grounds of this four-square-mile Christian retreat facility were breathtaking. With Howard acting as our guide for a brief tour of the place, BeBe and I kept elbowing each other and wondering what we'd gotten ourselves into. "Now, what did you say this place is?" I kept asking Howard as he ushered us through the foyer of the Grand Hotel and pointed out the fine shops and restaurants that were available for guests to enjoy. "It's a campground for Christians. Families come to relax, play, take in the sights, and worship." "A campground?" BeBe asked with surprise, looking at the luxurious surroundings. "Yes," Howard replied. "Mr. Bakker spent a lot of his boyhood attending campgrounds in Michigan." "This doesn't look like any of the camps our church took us to in Michigan when we were growing up," BeBe said, pointing out different things in amazement. "Evidently Mr. Bakker didn't go to the same camps that we went to," I chimed in. "Perhaps he did," Howard replied. "This place is what it is because he was disappointed with the camps he found in other places. You'll discover that the Bakkers are always building something."

"You have to see this place," I told my sisters and brothers on the telephone that first night away. "It's like we've died and gone to a heavenly camp meeting."

"Child, don't say that," Mom said, laughing as she unpacked some of our things. She and Dad had insisted upon flying down to Charlotte with us to inspect the place for themselves. So far, they were pleased. It appeared to be a clean, well-run Christian environment.

Howard was right. Jim Bakker had big dreams, and buildings would be going up and coming down throughout our time in North Carolina. The ministry was constantly growing and expanding. Convinced that people stopped going to campgrounds for summer vacations because of the dilapidated conditions of the buildings and grounds, the Bakkers wanted to build a vacation center where Christian families could come and be relaxed, spiritually and physically. Families could find at the Heritage USA comfortable lodgings with modern conveniences, a choice of places to eat right on the site, an array of activities like the amusement park and water towers for the children to enjoy, and places where parents and grandparents could shop, mill about, and attend worship. Many religious services took place throughout the week. Thousands of people from around the country and around the world visited Heritage USA every year. Something was always going on, enough to keep the crowds entertained: the nightly camp meetings, the daily teaching seminars, live music and singing, parades and plays on Main Street, prayer and communion services in the Upper Room, skits and performances in the beautiful outdoor setting of the Jerusalem amphitheater. People came from all over just to get a sight of the Bakkers, and whether they got their chance or not they had plenty of chances for relaxing and recreating on the beautiful and comfortable grounds of Heritage USA.

"You gotta give it to these people," remarked BeBe as we sat down to eat a first meal at one of the restaurants on the grounds. "They believe in going first class. They make it clear that Christians deserve the best."

"Makes you proud to be Christian," I added.

Our audition was on the day after our arrival. We spent the morning touring the television studio, which was equipped with all the up-to-date technology. It was an impressive sight. A couple of hundred people piled into the *PTL* studios, eager to be a part of the live television broadcast, which took place daily from the studios on the grounds. People crowded into the state-of-the-art television studio just to get a chance to glimpse the famous Jim and Tammy Faye Bakker and the famous celebrity Christian guests who came daily on the show. Four singers introduced as the *PTL* singers performed a couple of gospel numbers.

The auditions were after the morning broadcast. My brother and I were both nervous and giddy with excitement all morning. Howard was confident about our chances. He'd heard us perform with our brothers, The Winans, back in Detroit and was sure that we could blend in well with the *PTL* singers.

We almost weren't selected. I should say that BeBe is the one who almost didn't make it. He did something stupid which we would joke about for years afterward: He sang the wrong song—a song that didn't show his vocal ability. Thank God, Howard McCrary was one of the judges. His was the only familiar face in the studio as we stood before the camera to audition. BeBe and I were both nervous. For some reason, I went first. I felt like I was seven years old and back at the Mack Avenue Church of God in Christ. My throat was dry. I did the only thing I knew how to do, which was to close my eyes and sing a favorite song. I chose "Giver of Life," written by my brother Marvin, a song that was well suited for my vocal range. I also liked the words to the song.

Standing in front of a camera around strangers who were

deciding the fate of my career, I needed to be reminded whose hands I really was in, and who was the one able to give me what I needed right then. One Scripture that I often used to calm my nervousness was the New Testament book of James: "Every good and perfect gift is from above." I clung to that thought as I sang.

The next morning at the Sunday morning service on the campgrounds Howard asked me and BeBe to sing the hymn "Blessed Assurance." One minute into his ad lib of "Blessed Assurance" and it was obvious that BeBe had redeemed himself from his less-than-spectacular audition the day before. He sang like the musical genius I knew him to be. He was smooth as silk. He sang as though he was singing for his life.

"If we hadn't come up with another song for you, man, you'd be dead," Howard confided later. Everybody was laughing. We teased BeBe about bombing out on the first song. "I had to think of something quick to get you back in the running, man. So I figured we'd better go with what we know. And I knew that if Jim and Tammy heard you together they would go crazy, and it worked." Howard was right. After hearing us sing "Blessed Assurance" together, the Bakkers insisted that Howard hire us both as *PTL* singers.

❧ ❧

We will always have Howard to thank for giving us the chance to come to North Carolina and sing with the *PTL* singers. His quick thinking saved us. Singing "Giver of Life" showed the judges what they were looking for in my singing, but Howard saved *us*, and not just BeBe, because Howard knew that there was no way our parents would allow me to stay in North Carolina without my big brother. Joining that ministry was the opportunity of a lifetime. It gave us exposure, taught us priceless lessons, and allowed us to see a whole new world of music and the church.

7

PTL

❧ ❧

And I thank Christ Jesus our Lord who has enabled me,
because He counted me faithful, putting me into the ministry.
—1 Tim. 1:12

*P*eople at *PTL* were gracious
and accommodating. Everyone accepted and went out of their
way to make BeBe and me feel at home. The other six members of the *PTL* singers were glad to have us come on board.
The eight of us rehearsed long and hard hours in the beginning in order to blend our voices, to learn one another's range
and style, and in order to get to know one another. The work
was exhausting at times, but everyone was friendly and cooperative and acted as though they genuinely appreciated the
talents and sounds BeBe and I lent to the ensemble.

Admittedly, it was awkward and strange there in the beginning, especially for BeBe and me. It took us a while to get used to being around white people. There's no denying it: we had never before in our lives been around that many white people. We were not prejudiced. We were taught to love everybody and that everyone was equal. But it was . . . different.

Before *PTL* I had never really thought about the fact that I was a minority. I never felt as if I were part of a minority growing up in Detroit. But *PTL* gave me the opportunity to see the world differently. At *PTL* there was Howard, the musical director, one black male member of the orchestra, one black cameraman, BeBe and me. For the first time in my life I felt as though I had to represent the entire black race. The pressure was on to be excellent every day, at every performance. I became very self-conscious about my appearance. I wanted my hair to bounce and behave. And when it didn't, I was upset. Where did that come from? I felt that if I didn't have it all together, I was letting everyone in our race down. I was becoming a nervous wreck until finally I gave it over to God.

"Okay, God. You opened this door. You've got to settle my nerves and give me peace about who I am." Of course, God did. Eventually I began to relax and be myself. On the days when I thought everything went well—I looked good, I sounded good, I projected well—I gave praise to God. On the days when something was out of order and things fell through, I gave praise to God and said, "Oh well, there's always tomorrow."

We learned later that the Bakkers were in fact great fans of gospel music and that both had been influenced by Pentecostal worship and African-American music and worship styles as children of the South and in their travels throughout the South as a preaching and singing couple. BeBe and I were not the only black singers on their broadcast. Black celebrity singers and ministers were always being invited onto the broadcast. BeBe and I got a chance to meet and sing with people at *PTL* whose music we'd long admired, people like Pearl Bailey, Della Reese, Rosey Grier, Carlton Pearson, Candi Staton, and Jessie Dixon. I have to give Jim and Tammy Bakker credit for going out of their way on their broadcasts to make sure that black people were on the show. There was the normal amount of awkwardness and apprehension from some of their employees, of course. Trying to be nice and friendly, people sometimes said stupid things. Trying to go out of their way to prove they were not racist, some people exposed themselves in a racist manner. But all things considered, the atmosphere was kind and cooperative.

Singing at *PTL* expanded our horizons. We learned to accept that our way was not the only way to worship or to sing to God. This was my first time living and working up close with white people, and I learned a lot, not just about music and about other people. I learned a lot about myself also.

It helped that BeBe and I were working in a Christian environment. The fact that we were all Christians—or all wanted to be Christians—helped to ease tensions. After inflicting our daily share of thumps and bruises on one another with our quirky attitudes and homebred prejudices during work, thank God for the many worship services we shared together where we stood together with our hands lifted up in worship to God. And the inspiring messages of the Christian speakers who came on the broadcast revived us and reminded us of our true purpose. Eventually, those whose hearts were open to God and to the wooings of the Holy Spirit found their minds wandering back to transgressions committed against a coworker. By the end of the service, we were all hugging and kissing and begging one another's forgiveness and wishing to start over. As many times as we offended one another, we tried to forgive one another. That's one of the things I've always liked about working in a Christian organization. Christians aren't perfect, but a love for Jesus and a desire to live according to His teachings are apt to make you pause and take inventory of how you treat other people.

I learned at *PTL* that there are different faces of Christianity, and therefore, different ways of worshiping God. Everybody didn't believe the same way I believed, which was an eye-opener for me. One of my biggest shocks was learning that you could go to church for an hour! I was accustomed to going to church early in the mornings on Sunday and staying in church until late in the afternoon. I got acclimated to the one hour white people spend in worship and started teasing my family when I'd call back home to Detroit and find out that they'd just be getting back home from church at four o'clock. "You all just getting in?" I teased. "Lord, we have been home, child, taken a nap, eaten, and are on our way out to the park," I said, rubbing it in.

The faces and styles of worshiping God are different, but people themselves are not as different from one another as they think they are. After you peel back the traditions, mannerisms, habits, ingrained biases, and peculiar ways of doing things, you'll find that we're all pretty much the same. We laugh, we play, we love, we want to be happy, we weep, we bleed, we have our fears, we all want pretty much the same things: to love and to be loved.

Catch us at the right time or during the right season in our lives, and we're apt to show how really very curious we are about one another's ways of doing things.

❧ ❧

I thought that since I'd been taught to love everybody then I didn't have to worry about harboring any prejudices inside, but I was wrong. I'm just glad that I didn't let my prejudices prevent me from stepping outside the confines of my own limited thinking, risking new relationships, and making new friends. If I had, I would have missed out on

meeting and making some important and long-lasting relationships of my life.

In addition to me, the only black woman in the music
department at *PTL*, there were maybe one or two other black
females in the administrative department. I spent most of my
time with BeBe or alone. BeBe always made friends more
quickly than I did. He was always out visiting and having
new experiences. Once when Mom called to check on us, and
I told her that BeBe had gone with some friends white-water
rafting, she screamed, "That boy is from Detroit. He doesn't
know a thing about white-water rafting!" Her voice was laced
with real fear. "Try telling him that," I said. But Mom knew
BeBe. He is much like our father. He never meets someone
who doesn't become a friend, and he's always open to a new
adventure, and quick to take on new challenges. I've looked
like a wallflower around him.

When I wasn't at work or checking out Charlotte with
BeBe, I was home in the apartment I shared with my brother.
The other female *PTL* singers were friendly and often invited
me to join them on different occasions, but I was a loner. The
truth is that I was lonely for a black community. I missed
church, even the long exciting services. For a time there it
was so bad that the sight of a Denny's commercial on the television would almost send me into tears. Back in Detroit our
family and friends hung out at Denny's all the time. I missed
the soul-to-soul conversations that sisters and girlfriends are

In the beginning... as Baby Priscilla, at just 8 ½ months.

Good times during the summer of '69, all of four years old.
Top: Baby-sitting our baby siblings. That's me on the right, holding
my sister Angie, at the house of our friends the Ewings.
Bottom: At a big birthday bash. I'm in the center with the party hat and
pigtails—as my brothers and sisters would say,
always the center of attention.

My brother Daniel and I as junior attendants in our cousin's wedding. Don't we look grown up?

Here I am, three times over, in my school picture from the first grade.

My graduation picture, 1980— ready to go out and take on the world!

BeBe and I at our first recording session with the amazing Whitney Houston. We were recording "Hold Up the Light," which became one of BeBe and my signature songs.

Right: BeBe and I in one of our most fun appearances—on Sesame Street, *with another well-known duo, Bert and Ernie.*

Below: My fairy-tale wedding on June 23, 1984. Part of what made it so special was having all my brothers and sisters sharing my wedding with me.

*My husband, Alvin, a[nd]
I at the exquisite thirtie[th]
birthday party BeBe
threw for me in 1994.*

*This lovely man is
Pastor Jesse T. Stacks of
Shalom Temple, ordained
by my grandfather just
before his death, who was
my pastor from infancy
into adulthood.*

Sister Kiwanis Hockett and Pastor Horace of the Born Again Non-Denominational Church in Nashville, Tennessee, where my family and I attend church.

Two of my favorite people in the world—my grandparents, Grandad Howze and Grandma Laura.

Here is the whole gang, in 1992. Standing, left to right: Daniel, David, Carvin, Ronald, Marvin, Michael, and BeBe; middle: Mom and Dad; seated: Debbie, me, and Angie. (AMEEN HOWRANI)

*The soul of our family, my mom and dad, at a photo shoot
for their most recent album. They've recorded two!*

*At the Dove Awards in 1996, with my two awards from that year.
One was for Female Vocalist of the Year—it was my first Dove Award
and I was the first African American to ever win it!* (PATTY MASTEN)

Here I am with my first Grammy as a solo artist—for my album
Alone in His Presence—*which I won at the 1996 Grammy Awards,*
where I also performed.

With lovely lady Rosie O'Donnell, who had me on her show after I won the Dove and Grammy awards. I performed, we had a wonderful time chatting, and she even sent presents home to Alvin III and Ashley! (LEIGH ANN HARDIE, SPARROW RECORDS)

Alvin and I with President and Mrs. Clinton after the 1996 Christmas in Washington *television special. What a treat that was!* (DIANA WALKER)

*With the fabulous Oprah Winfrey at the Essence Awards in April
1997, where Oprah hosted and I performed.*
(ROBERT SHANKLIN/CAPITAL ENTERTAINMENT)

*This was one of my favorite events—when I performed at the
Songwriters Hall of Fame induction ceremony in June 1998. We did
a tribute to Diana Ross, who was being presented with a lifetime
achievement award, and rubbed elbows with some wonderful people,
including (opposite page): Berry Gordy (top left) and Paul Simon
(top right)* (ROBERT SHANKLIN/CAPITAL ENTERTAINMENT)

Left to right: Leslie Uggams, Berry Gordy, Diana Ross, me, Valerie Simpson, and Marilyn McCoo. (PHOTOS BY ROBERT SHANKLIN/CAPITAL ENTERTAINMENT)

My beautiful family: Alvin II, Alvin III, Ashley, and I in our
1998 Christmas family photo. They are what makes it all worthwhile!

apt to have. Living and working with your brother just isn't the same. BeBe was too busy moving, traveling, and venturing out into different things, leaving me behind in our apartment to watch TV and to mope. I could have gotten angry with him. But I didn't. Although there is no denying that I was lonely, I also enjoyed the quiet and the privacy. It reminded me of the time when I played with my dolls for hours on end.

After only a few months, however, I wanted to go home.

❧ ❧

Learning to sing in front of white audiences was by far one of the hardest things to adjust to. I'd never sung before such quiet audiences before. We could be up onstage singing our hearts out, but the audiences never gave us an ounce of support. Not an "Amen" in the place. No "Praise the Lord." Not even a "Sing children!" as we might have gotten back at Shalom Temple in Detroit. Not a whimper of feedback. "God, I must have been awful out there," BeBe whispered to me when he'd finished one of his numbers. "If you were awful, then I must have bombed yesterday when they did the same thing to me," I replied. For weeks in the beginning we walked around feeling kind of disappointed. Eventually it dawned on both of us that it wasn't us. We were in a different environment.

White church audiences are different from black audiences,

at least they were back then when we first started off at *PTL*. Now on religious broadcasts you can see as many whites as blacks waving their hands and wiping tears from their faces during worship services. But that was not our experience at *PTL* back in the early 1980s. We missed the way black audiences let you know that they are with you in a song through their smiles, nods, waves, or by standing up in the middle of the song yelling "Sing, CeCe!" or "Sing that song, BeBe!" White audiences back then, and still some today, were apt to sit silently. A warm and generous applause after the song was all you could expect. But their silence was not to be taken as a lack of emotion.

Often it wasn't until after the daily broadcasts, when we were all piling out of the television studio, that invariably members of the audience lingered behind to let one of us know what a particular song meant to them. "I can't tell you how much that song touched my heart, young lady," one of them might say with tears in his or her eyes. BeBe and I were taken completely off guard the first time this happened to one of us. They accosted us in the parking lot, wanting to shake our hand or give us a hug for one of the songs. Just the same, it was always good to have speckles of black people from time to time show up as a part of the television audience at *PTL*. We could always count on them for an occasional hand wave or "Amen" when the *PTL* singers sang.

Only once in my three years at *PTL* did I witness an

audience full of black people on the campgrounds. Evangelist R. R. Schambach came to PTL for a camp meeting, and the *PTL* singers were singing. That night the auditorium was full of black people. I couldn't believe my eyes. I didn't know that so many black people were in Charlotte. They came in droves that night, and I was so happy and excited to be back in a sea of black faces.

❧ ❧

Singing without my big family was perhaps the hardest adjustment. We were accustomed to singing with the whole family. Now it was just BeBe and me and the other *PTL* singers. BeBe and I had to learn how to sing alone. I learned my own strengths and weaknesses; when there's no one around to back you, it's good to know what you can and can't do. Focusing as we had to on the tiny camera lens, and pretending we were looking into the eyes of a stadium of people taught me how to sing my praises to God.

One of the things I learned about myself was that when it came to my interactions with women at *PTL*, I'm afraid I let my own prejudices—the catty female prejudices women sometimes are guilty of when dealing with one another—keep me from jumping out there and making friends. Fortunately, there was one young white woman who wouldn't let me stay in my shell too long. Penny Hollenbeck was too down-to-earth, too friendly, and too stubborn to let me get away with being distant. Every morning at nine, when it was time for our wardrobes to be fitted, Penny greeted me with a great big smile and tried to strike up a friendly chatter with me about one thing or another. At first, I was convinced she wasn't someone I wanted to be with. Although she was attractive, she didn't look sincere, I told myself. Just looking at her, I decided that her warmth was an act. She thinks she's cute, I said to myself. In actuality, she was and still is; but I couldn't imagine being friends with her. I refused every invitation she extended to me. I'd settled in to being by myself there in Charlotte, certain that no one really wanted to be my friend. I was in fact too scared and shy to step outside my shell. And I almost let my prejudices and insecurities lock me in. Thank God, Penny was a sincere Christian. She wouldn't take no as an answer from me.

"So, what do you do when you're not singing?" she asked, pretending not to notice the barrier I kept up—not caring.

"Oh, just things," I said.

"What kind of things?" she asked. She insisted upon talking. She was too down-to-earth to let me keep up my barrier.

"Just things," I repeated.

"If you ever want to go out to the movies, or out shopping, I'll be happy to take you around. You must be dying to get out and do some shopping." Was she making a crack about my clothes? I couldn't be sure. If she was, her pleasant expression never changed as she continued to outfit me in whatever we were supposed to wear that day.

Every day I was pleasant but remained standoffish. She and BeBe hit it right off. Which didn't help things in my mind. After being around her constantly I discovered that Penny was delightful—relaxed, easy-going. Best of all, she was outgoing and crazy. Which was just fine with BeBe, who was also outgoing and crazy. I didn't want to be left out of the fun, and I was tired of hiding behind a shield of catty suspicions. Underneath it all, I needed a friend. I remember one night when the three of us laughed and talked as though we'd known one another all our lives. We exchanged tales about families back home, people we'd gone to school with, high school mischief we barely escaped, and rumors circulating around *PTL*.

Pretty soon Penny became my first white friend. I was so wrong about her, totally wrong. I still don't remember what exactly made me let her into my life. Perhaps it was because it was clear that this tall blond girl from Binghamton, New York, didn't have any hang-ups about being around black people. It neither fascinated her, nor did it make her uptight. People were people to her, which made it easy to relax with her. We tease each other about all this now, seventeen years later. We agree that the friendship was sealed when we started doing each other's hair. That's always a true sign that women have bonded. Discovering that I'd spent some time in cosmetology school, Penny complained that she needed some help with her hair and asked if I could help her. I laughed and assured her that fixing blond hair was not part of my training, but I would do my best. I took her blond mane in my hands and put it up into a sweeping French roll that was flattering and attractive for her looks. It wasn't until later that I discovered that when she was trying to get me to talk in wardrobe, she was looking for a female roommate. We started teasing each other that if I hadn't been so stuck up, I could have gotten her for a roommate instead of BeBe. Boy, did I blow it. Penny was so cool, so street, so comfortable to be around, and so funny. Why did I let my prejudices almost keep me from a woman who has been now for seventeen years a friend of easy laughter? The only real way to break down barriers is to get to know each other a little.

My own loneliness and need for friendship made me alert and sensitive to the same need in other people. In the three years I was at *PTL* it was evident to me that Tammy Faye Bakker needed a friend. Unfortunately, I was not to be that friend. I was just an employee, one of the singers in the *PTL* ensemble, and some twenty years Tammy Faye's junior. But I knew a troubled woman when I saw one, and Tammy Faye Bakker was going through a lot in those days. My heart and prayers went out to her every day. I know now from some of the revelations about the Bakkers that have come out since the demise of *PTL* that Tammy's mood swings on the set of *PTL* were probably the result of her insecurities. Some days, she would bounce onto the set in the best of moods: friendly, perky, relaxed, and outgoing. Other days, she came in withdrawn, distracted, tense, and irritable.

I could sometimes tell by how much makeup she was wearing how she was feeling. It seemed that on the days she was at her lowest, her makeup was the heaviest. Years later, after I'd left *PTL* and was traveling and singing around the country garnering awards and publicity, I understood better how some women use makeup to hide behind and put distance between them and the outside world, much like the way some people use dark shades to cover their eyes and hide the fact that they have been crying.

With life's knocks and bruises awaiting me down the road when I launched my own career as a singer, I would have a chance to discover this firsthand for myself.

Actually, singing together was the furthest thing from our minds when BeBe and I moved to North Carolina. We thought we were going to be part of an ensemble. People think that just because we are sister and brother, we started off singing together. Very few people know that Tammy Faye Bakker was the one who introduced the song to BeBe and me that would eventually become our signature duet on *PTL* broadcasts. "Lord, Lift Us Up" would eventually become one of the most frequently requested songs by *PTL* audiences. Howard paired us to sing together from time to time before "Lord, Lift Us Up," but after we started singing that song we couldn't get away from each other. "Lord, Lift Us Up" was a favorite of both Jim and Tammy Faye Bakker. Recorded by Joe Crocker and Jennifer Warnes as part of the soundtrack for the movie *An Officer and a Gentleman*, the song was originally titled, "Love Lifts Us Up." But when Tammy Faye heard the song she was so convinced that it was meant to be a Christian song that she rewrote some of the words to the song and convinced Howard to teach it to the *PTL* singers. The name was changed to "Lord, Lift Us Up," and BeBe and I were chosen as the lead singers. It was an instant hit on the *PTL* broadcasts.

BeBe and I ended up singing duet because requests started pouring into the station for us to sing together. People liked to hear that brother-and-sister pair sing together. Churches throughout the country started calling the network inviting the two "colored" singers, BeBe and CeCe, to come to their church to sing together for one or another of their church programs. Pretty soon, we couldn't get through a day of broadcasting without singing that song. People in the audience, people throughout the country, especially Jim and Tammy Faye—everyone was always asking us to sing that song together.

You can imagine the stir that our being singled out for special performances began to create in the *PTL* ensemble. The other members tried to act as if it didn't matter, but there was no hiding the growing weariness among some of them. We were tired of singing the song ourselves. I tried not to notice the resentment I was sometimes feeling from some of the members. I had learned long ago from singing in church that you can't apologize for God's plan. You can't explain why and how God uses you to communicate to an audience. It's the Lord's work.

Had we not had each other to lean on, BeBe and I might not have made it for those three years. It was good to have each other to bounce things off of, and to keep each other company. How many times at night we sat around and thought back to those times Mom, Dad, and our siblings stayed up laughing with one another. Enjoying each other's company, we were grateful we had a close-knit family. We thanked our parents for making us stay close to each other. We'd always been close as the seventh and eighth children in the family, with a mere two years between us. But living and working together in North Carolina, just the two of us, we became closer than we'd every been before. We depended upon each other, even though our personalities are as different as night and day. I am calm and laid back, much like Mom, whereas BeBe, like Dad, is hyperactive and impulsive. He claims that I think too long about things and that my wait-and-see attitude only results in missed opportunities. I complain that he is generous to a fault and jumps before he thinks.

BeBe was always dragging people into our apartment in Charlotte for a meal, to sleep over, or just to hang out. He's always been a sucker for a hard-luck story. "Are you crazy bringing this person into this apartment?" I'd yell. "We don't know him."

"But he works for the studio. He's cool," BeBe would say.

"Regardless, we don't know him, BeBe." I would be steaming by now. "Get him out right this minute."

BeBe and I have always had totally different notions about home, which may sound strange since we had grown up in the very same household. For me, growing up in a family of ten children made me relish the quiet of our tiny apartment. Home is where you go when you want to peel away the emotions of the day, where you rest and kick back, where you get to be alone and relax in your own private rituals. BeBe, on the other hand, missed the noise and commotion of having six brothers and three sisters around the house; home wasn't home for him unless there was a bunch of people around making noise and getting in the way. I spent quite a few nights in our North Carolina apartment locked behind my bedroom door, angry and stewing in my own juices. My bedroom was the only place where I could get the peace I longed for. If ever our differences became too great, one of us would call home for intermediation. Mom or Dad would get on the phone and talk sense into one of us and remind us that we were family and needed to work things out. Luckily, those times were few, and we were able to work out our differences. We never held grudges or stopped talking—for long. Eventually, one of us would do something to make the other laugh, or someone at work would do something that one of us couldn't wait to tell the other about, and things would return to normal between us.

After all, we were family.

છે છે

Growing up in a church where there are very definite notions of what is right and wrong, where you hear regularly about hell and God's wrath, where there is much quoting of the verse that says, "The wages of sin is death, but the gift of God is eternal life," you're always on the lookout for any trace of sin in your life. Pentecostals have a laundry list of sins that are to be avoided. First, there are the God-given ones that everyone knows about: lying, stealing, killing, gambling, fornicating, adultery, gossiping, and taking God's name in vain. Then there are the human ones, which vary from religious tradition to religious tradition. In my church, these include going to the movies, wearing makeup, wearing jewelry, wearing open-toe shoes, and painting your fingernails. I have managed to avoid most of them on the major list. But I tried a few on the human list and discovered that when I opened my eyes, God had not struck me down. Not only that, I enjoyed the experience. The first one was going to the movies. I don't know how I let my coworkers at *PTL* talk me into going to the movies. BeBe had gone to his first movie a few weeks before and returned to the apartment boasting about the experience, so I thought I might give it a try. *Tootsie* was my first movie, and it was great!

My job at *PTL* required BeBe and me to wear some strange and outlandish costumes sometimes—rodeo clothes, long colonial dresses, clown outfits—for parades and broadcast segments that centered around a particular theme. While I knew I looked stupid, and I was always uncomfortable in many of those outfits, I didn't go so far as to think it was a sin to be seen in any of them, but persuading me to wear makeup on my face was something different.

"Now, CeCe, girl, I don't mean you any harm, but you are going to have to do better," Howard's wife, Shay, said, pulling me aside one afternoon in the studio after rehearsal.

"What do you mean?" I couldn't imagine what she was talking about.

"Girl, have you seen yourself on the monitor?"

"Yes. What's the problem?" I liked Shay a lot. She was cool and was known for speaking her mind. She was also a great cook. That girl could rattle some pots and pans, as they say. I never wanted to be on her bad side. The girl cooked too good not to be invited to her dinner table.

"CeCe girl, you would be ravishing if you'd put a little powder on so you could hide your blemishes and cut down on some of that shine on your face. And, honey, a little mascara would bring out the natural beauty of those sultry eyes that you have."

"But Shay—"

"Wait. I'm not finished," she said, reaching into her pocketbook. She fumbled through it, looking for something. "I have just the right shade of lipstick for those lips of yours." She pulled the cap off a tiny metal tube.

"Girl, I can't wear that stuff." I stepped back in horror. "My mother and grandmother would die if they caught me with my face all painted. It's a sin!" I cried.

Shay laughed. "Says who?"

"Says the Bible."

"Where in the Bible?"

"Er . . . um . . . I don't know where, but I know it's in there." My mind was racing. I tried to remember the passage. Shay was a very attractive woman who, despite the conservative religious background we shared, did not have some of the same hang-ups I had. She was a serious shopper. And she knew how to coordinate her shoes with her dresses, and her dresses with her lipstick and her lipstick with her eye shadow. It was apparent that she had shed some of what she thought were man-made teachings on the way women should dress and behave. She was sharp, witty, and intelligent.

"You find where it says that women aren't supposed to wear makeup and bring the passage to me, and I'll leave you alone. But if it's not there then let's see what we can do about enhancing that pretty face of yours."

I had my ammunition from the book of Timothy when I saw her that evening:

> *In like manner, women [should] adorn themselves in modest apparel, with shamefacedness and sobriety, not with braided hair, or gold, or pearls or costly array, but (which becometh women professing godliness) with good works.*

"Be real, CeCe. Where does it say anything about makeup?" Shay fired back.

"It doesn't have to," I responded.

"It admonishes women to be modest and decent," Shay replied. "It doesn't say you can't wear makeup, CeCe."

"How can I go on national TV singing praises to God looking like a Jezebel?" I tried not to show my own amusement at the question.

"You're not going to look like a Jezebel when I finish with you," she said, pulling out a makeup case the size of most women's pocketbooks. "I'm just going to see to it that a modest and decent amount of powder, rouge, lipstick, and mascara is applied to your face to help you look better for the camera. We want the world to know that just because you're saved doesn't mean you have to look homely."

"You're trying to say I look bad?" I said, pretending to pout.

"No, I'm just trying to say that God is not opposed to your looking great. Now get in that room," Shay said, shoving me into the bathroom and in front of a mirror. "While we're at it, let's see what kind of earrings we can put on you."

"Jesus, have mercy on my soul" is the prayer I whispered as my eyes fell on the assortment of makeup and jewelry Shay had for me to choose from.

I was growing up right before my own eyes—living and working away from home, making my own money, coming and going as I pleased. Since *Tootsie*, I was going to the movies whenever something clean and respectable was showing. Now I was wearing makeup, earrings, and eventually pants. I was really testing boundaries, discovering for myself what things I, Priscilla "CeCe" Winans, thought were inviolable and dear to my soul and what things I respected, but no longer held as sacred.

I still had boundaries: sins like drinking, cursing, and sleeping around were out of the question. But I discovered that it was possible to love and work with people who were totally different from me. I went out with Christian singers who were in town appearing on the broadcast, well-known artists whose notions of a good time differed from my own. I loved and respected these singers, and I *loved* their music, but I still ordered a soda, resisted the sanctified urge to judge, and found that I could still enjoy the evening, laughing and sharing with many of them.

BeBe thought the new me looked wonderful. "Thank God," he said when he first saw me. I liked my new look. I also liked the tiny steps of freedom I was beginning to take. I got over the guilt. I could feel God doing something new in me.

⋘ ⋙

Over the years since leaving *PTL*, people have tried time and time again to get me to say negative things about my years at *PTL*, but I refuse to do it. For one thing, nothing negative comes to mind. Working at *PTL* for almost three years was one of the best things that ever happened to me. It opened my life and my ministry to a whole new world. I met so many special people during my days there, people who would be important to me later on, when BeBe and I would leave and begin our own singing careers. The Bakkers gave BeBe and me our first big break in singing.

Rumors were always flying around the studios about infidelity, drugs, embezzlement, and some takeover, but that wasn't anything new to either BeBe or me. We'd grown up in the black church, where rumors of sex, lies, and scandals were always floating around. People are the same everywhere. We all make mistakes.

We joined a ministry when we signed on to work at *PTL*. Despite all the excesses and abuses that have been uncovered and splashed across the headlines since we left, it can't be denied that a lot of good came out of Jim and Tammy Faye's dreams and work through *PTL* and Heritage USA. People were blessed, spirits were lifted, and lives were changed through that ministry, including our lives. Thousands of workers poured their hearts into that ministry, working from sunup to sundown, praying over every detail, trying to render a godly service to everyone who came through the doors. We were all hurt and devastated when the ministry fell apart.

With the highly publicized trial, the tragic breakup of Jim and Tammy Faye's marriage, the dissolution of their ministries, and the dismantling of the *PTL* ministries, a lot of people were hurt and a lot of dreams were shattered.

I left *PTL* to pursue other interests a few years before the seams at *PTL* began to unravel. I knew that the Lord was calling me to other things. But the lessons and memories I stored in my heart from those three years in Charlotte would be a benefit for me and serve me for the rest of my life.

I can't think of anything bad to say about Jim Bakker,

and I wouldn't even if I knew anything. I never got close enough to him or the inner workings of the ministry to have any firsthand knowledge of any unsavory actions. All I know is that the Bakkers were two wonderful people who, like all of us, made their share of mistakes.

More than twelve years after leaving *PTL*, and two years after Jim Bakker's release from prison, the two of us shared the pulpit one Sunday afternoon at a church in Atlanta. I was there to sing, and Jim had been asked to speak about the lessons of his life. That day, he'd also been asked to introduce me as one of his former *PTL* singers. Seeing him that afternoon, for the first time in more than ten years, brought back a flood of memories that threatened to overwhelm me and keep me from regaining my composure. I thanked him for his support when we hugged, and he thanked me for my prayers and told me how proud he was of the way the Lord had been guiding both BeBe's and my careers since our days at *PTL*. We hugged there on that Atlanta pulpit, and our admiration for each other was evident to all.

His introduction was kind, and it was obvious that the memories of the good he'd tried to accomplish at *PTL* is what had remained uppermost on his mind. That the Lord had used his ministry to help BeBe and I get our first start and to launch our careers was obviously very gratifying to him. He had followed our careers and was proud of the opportunity to introduce me that evening. The years had been kind to Jim Bakker, despite the shame and humiliation he had suffered. His hair was a lot grayer, to be sure, and he'd obviously experienced God in prison in a way that was greater than he ever had at *PTL*. He hadn't lost the sweet boyish grin that could make one relax and be comfortable in his presence. In his introduction he asked me if I would take him back to sweeter times in his life by singing one of my old *PTL* songs that remained a favorite of his, "Blessed, Broken, and Given."

> *"After my blessing, after my breaking,*
> *Let me given to bring sight to all men.*
> *Lord bless me and break me again and again . . ."*

The past ten years of his life had become much like the communion bread the song commemorates. He had gone from being blessed to being broken, to seeing all the ministries and fortunes he'd amassed lost and given away, to then being blessed by becoming now a blessing to God's people by sharing his broken experiences as a lesson for all.

⧉ ⧉

Standing before Jim Bakker that day in Atlanta, singing a song that held special significance for both of us, reminded me why I have always insisted upon catching a red-eye flight back home after all the award ceremonies are over. I know firsthand how easy it is to become so drunk by this carousel called stardom, so dazed by your own ambitions, hungry for the next conquest, that you lose sight of what's really important. Christians can get so caught up in the business that they can neglect their spiritual needs. When that happens, we become vulnerable. The business world is a beast with its own life force, forever threatening to suck you up into its belly of obligations, opportunities, and distractions.

I've always been afraid that if I ever look straight and long at the tiny camera lens in the studio and into the bright lights, if I really begin to read my own press, if I ever get caught up in the glitter and glamour of being a singer and a star, then I might lose my way and my purpose. I might get so far out there that I might not be able to find my way back. I pray to God that before that ever happens, I can get on a red-eye and come home to my family.

PTL

A place for everyone to come and see
people of every color, race, or creed.
To be blessed, relax and enjoy the fun,
where you could always hear God's praises being sung.
It's where I started my journey,
it was a new beginning of answering my call;
a platform for the world to see
the special gift God had given me.

I didn't know at the time why I was sent to this strange land,
but when I look back I can clearly see
my steps were ordered; it was God's place.
"Lord Lift Us Up Where We Belong" was the song we sang,
it gave us national exposure and led the way to fame.
PTL once a reality, now seems like only a dream,
a dream that gave life, hope, love, and allowed me the
    chance to sing.
A dream that will last forever because it birthed
    beautiful things.

8

Love

Wherefore they are no more two,
but one flesh.
—*Matt. 19:6*

*W*hen visitors to *PTL* asked
me whether I was from North Carolina, I was careful to reply,
"I live in North Carolina, but my home is Detroit." The distinction was important to me. I never got used to living in
North Carolina, even though people in the state had no problem claiming me as their own. Whenever I'd walk through my
apartment complex, to and from the laundry facilities, or go to
the malls to shop, people were always coming up to me
because they recognized me from the broadcasts. When I first
saw myself on television, I had to pinch myself. "Wait a

minute," I said to BeBe. "We're on television!" It was a powerful realization: television could get God's message across to
hundreds of thousands of people across the land.

Learning to focus my singing on the tiny television camera lens was difficult. You can fool yourself into thinking that
you're playing make-believe and no one is really looking, but
try going out to the 7-Eleven in the middle of the night with
your hair in rollers and you'll find out that the world knows
you. I thought that since I lived in the small town of
Charlotte, no one knew me, but I was wrong.

Charlotte was too tame for my northern city-girl tastes. I
was a Detroit girl. Admittedly, it was nice to live in a place
where people walked down the streets without fear and felt
comfortable not locking their front doors. But Charlotte was
too quiet, even for my tastes. In Detroit there was electricity
in the air, even when just traveling between home, church,
and school. People were always milling about. Music was
always blasting from some radio or tape deck somewhere.
Cars were backed up on the highway. You could be sure
you'd be able to buy a fish sandwich or a Twinkie somewhere
in the city as late as midnight. All the stores in Charlotte
closed early. We had to go miles to find a black church. We
were starving for color. We were desperate to soak up some
black culture and to eat soul food.

I loved my work at *PTL*, but as often as I could I got on a
plane and headed back to Detroit. I have always been a

homebody—I still am. I missed my mother's cooking. I missed being razzed by my older brothers. And no matter where I move to in the world, home will always be wherever Mom and Dad live. What's more, I needed to go to the beauty parlor so I could get my hair done up right. Everyone knows that some of the best black hairstylists in the world are in Detroit! Hairstylists at *PTL* were clueless about what to do with a black woman's hair. Lord, I missed black culture.

Part of the joy of coming home was in getting to tag along with my siblings to the many outings the young people at church sponsored. One weekend everybody was going bowling. So, off to the young people's outing I went, and I'm glad I did. It was at this outing that I met my future husband.

At first, I thought the dark, handsome young guy with the serious eyes was my friend Sabrina's boyfriend. Thinking back on it, Alvin had an easy comfortable manner with everyone. It was obvious that everyone knew him except me. I discovered later that he wasn't Sabrina's boyfriend. Alvin Love had the warmest smile in the world, and he was the most handsome guy at the bowling alley. I couldn't help but notice him. He was a new member of Shalom Temple and had joined the church a few months earlier, which made him something of a mystery to everyone. Whenever a single man joins a church, the single women in the church circle him like sharks. I thought he was cute, but I was home only for the weekend. The last thing on my mind was a relationship. I certainly didn't have the time to be in a relationship. I was too busy singing and traveling. Besides, I was only eighteen at the time. I knew how crazy women act over a good-looking single man. I had had plenty of experience observing the way women act around good-looking available men. Watching girls throw themselves at my brothers I'd always promised myself that I wouldn't be a silly woman and would never chase a man. I wasn't thinking about changing my life's direction. I was on my way back to North Carolina to my ministry of singing at *PTL* after the weekend was over.

I was used to guys at the church admiring me from afar, but that was as much romance as I ever experienced. The few who mustered the nerve to strike up a conversation eventually lost their nerve along the way when they were reminded of all the brothers I had. But this one was different.

After that night at the bowling alley, Alvin and I saw each other again the next evening at church. We exchanged greetings and a few courtesies, but nothing more. Some months later, however, on July 4, 1983, to be exact, my brother Ronald flew down to North Carolina with a stranger in tow. Ronald along with my other three brothers who made up The Winans were scheduled to make an appearance on *PTL*. I was surprised to see the friend Ronald brought along! It was the guy from the bowling alley. He said that Ronald had invited him to tag along, believing that he would enjoy the trip and change of scenery. Thinking back on it, I'm certain that Ronald was up to his famous matchmaking game, and Alvin was all for it. At the time, however, I was clueless.

We had a great weekend together, BeBe, Marvin, Carvin, Ronald, Michael, Alvin, friends, other family members and myself. It was good to have my family with me in North Carolina. Everybody laughed and acted crazy. Alvin and I got to spend time together. We strolled the *PTL* grounds, we went on rides in the Carowinds Amusement Park, we laughed, teased, and we talked and talked. Ronald thought we looked cute together. It was apparent to everyone that something special was in the air. I knew if he could survive my brothers' badgering he was tough. The night before he and Ronald were scheduled to go back to Detroit, Alvin phoned from the hotel, saying he needed to see me. I couldn't refuse him. I could barely sleep thinking about him. I kept thinking about the way he made me feel. I felt relaxed around him, as though I had known him all my life. Whatever discomfort I did feel was not the result of anything Alvin did, but the result of my lack of experience with potential suitors. One moment I was fretting about the way I looked, the next moment I was marveling at how safe and secure I felt around him. By the time Alvin called me that night from the hotel where he was staying and asked to see me, I was dreading the fact that he would have to leave.

Ronald and Alvin came over to my apartment. Ronald sat in the living room while Alvin and I sat in the dining area. I could tell by the way he was looking that he was about to get serious. I was scared about what he was getting ready to say. He didn't have to call me to come out in the night to tell me that he'd had a wonderful time, but . . . I knew there must have been something more, but I didn't know what.

"Marriage is very sacred to me," he began. "Oh no," I thought. "Don't tell me . . ."

He began to tell me his whole life story, why he had never married, the kind of woman he'd been searching for, the great time he'd had with me and my family over the weekend. He ended with the words: ". . . and I feel that you're the person I want to marry."

My mind was whirling. The man doesn't waste any words!

"I'm really not thinking about marriage right now, Alvin," I said, trying to sound nonchalant. But I doubt that I succeeded. Never let him see you sweat, right? I could barely contain myself. I could have jumped and screamed with joy. But I remained calm and cool. At eighteen going on nineteen, the furthest thing from my mind was marriage. But I couldn't deny that I was interested, very interested.

Alvin smiled. "Let's just see what happens. Can I call you when I get home? Can we just say that we'll stay in touch?" he pleaded.

"Sure," I whispered.

"Oh *Al*vin . . ." BeBe and all my friends at *PTL* couldn't wait to tease me about the way I called Alvin's name. "Oh, *Al*vin this . . . Oh, *Al*vin that." The moment Ronald and Alvin pulled off on their way back to Detroit, BeBe was on my case.

I just chuckled and brushed him off. "Boy, be quiet."

Perhaps what I was feeling was or wasn't written all over my face, but it was surely written all over my heart. I was so happy. I couldn't think of anything or anyone but Alvin. I missed him the moment the car pulled away. I couldn't believe this was happening to me. I was only eighteen years old. I was finally beginning to get settled in North Carolina, finally beginning to resign myself to being alone, and now a long-distance love had come along.

How do you explain falling in love? It's like trying to explain what it feels like to fall off a cliff or jump off a plane thousands of miles in the air. How do you explain the sensation of falling and falling and falling and never hitting the bottom? It's simultaneously the most terrifying and the most exhilarating experience of your life. I knew the moment Alvin and Ronald pulled away in their car that I was in the throes of a free fall.

Only God could save me now.

Alvin and I talked on the telephone every day. We made dates to see each other. He came down to Charlotte as often as his job at Xerox allowed him. I went up to Detroit as often as my singing and traveling permitted. More and more requests were pouring into *PTL* now for BeBe and I to come and sing at churches and ceremonies. Before they had been exciting, but now they were making life complicated. I knew I couldn't stay at home all day waiting for Alvin's phone calls, I had a ministry to keep together. BeBe was complaining that I was always on the phone too much. Our phone bills were enormous! It got so bad that BeBe just started asking for my entire payroll check.

❧ ❧

Singing together was still new for BeBe and me. At first, we didn't know how to handle these requests. Before coming to North Carolina, we'd never sung together as a duet. The songs we did together on the *PTL* broadcast were always at Howard's or Tammy Faye's request, which meant that all we had to do was sing what was put in front of us. But when people started inviting us to come and sing, we had to come up with our own material. We'd choose material on a hunch that it would work—"Okay, you sing this part, and I'll sing this part"—and off we went to perform with a track tape. We were inventing ourselves as we went along. Pretty soon, family and friends back home were calling us "the black Donny and Marie Osmond." The Osmonds were the only other brother-and-sister team people were acquainted with, so the comparison was inevitable. We didn't know what God was doing with us. We just wanted to get out and stretch our vocal chords.

It was a struggle to fit a long-distance romance into my busy schedule. Worse yet, it was expensive staying on the phone all night. But I loved every minute of it. Alvin and I had agreed to seek God about our relationship. If God was in it, we knew He would make it possible for us to find ways to see each other. The reality is that we were filled with apprehension. I, for one, didn't want to be blind. I prayed every day: "Lord, if this is what You want for me, let me know. If this isn't Your perfect will for my life, I don't want it. I can't see ten years from now. I don't want to end up in some divorce court." Alvin was praying his own similar prayers, I later discovered.

It was obvious that moving to Charlotte gave me the freedom to experience everything that was forbidden to me when I had lived in my parents' home. Coworkers were always inviting me to go out with them. My friend Penny always knew about the latest excitement in Charlotte and was always trying to get me to go out and have some fun. But I was always reluctant.

I have always been scared to jump into things. "God, is this the right thing to do?" "God, show me the right way." "God, You know I want to be in Your will." Normally, I don't move unless I'm convinced I have God's permission. It's not that I'm fanatical or anything. Nor have I lived the life of a saint. Give me a Bible, a bed, and a twenty-four-inch television screen, and I'm pretty happy. "Scaredy cat" my brothers called me when we were growing up, and they were partly right. Although I never admitted it to them. "The truth is that CeCe has an old soul," as Grandmother Howze would point out. I study people and try to learn from their mistakes. Coworkers sometimes snickered behind my back that I was boring, that I never wanted to have fun, but the truth is that I never wanted to have their kind of fun. Since my days selling hot dogs at Coney Island in Detroit, I have worked. And work is what I have always done in order to have my own money and to keep myself preoccupied. It's all I ever saw my parents do, besides go to church. We had to do without so many things when I was growing up that working became the way for me to see other parts of the world. I can throw myself into my work, work through the night, and never come up for air. And when I do, I want to come home to family and very close friends and relax, look at TV, make popcorn, watch old movies.

I loved my work at *PTL* even though things were sometimes hectic there. There were the rehearsals. There were the live broadcasts. There were the rumors. There were the special appearances. There were the parades that we had to take part in, and the evening worship services, where we sometimes had to sing. And there was all that traveling around the country. I felt blessed to be a part of the ministry. I felt blessed to have a job that paid me to sing with my brother, blessed to have a job that paid me to do the one thing in life I loved the most, which was singing. I didn't know how long God meant for me to be in North Carolina or where I would go next, but I knew that I was blessed for having come this far.

But I realized that being paid for singing and having the opportunity to sing before a national audience were not validation that I was living my purpose. My real validation was in enjoying my work and finding joy and contentment in it. I knew that when these two were gone, it would be time to go—despite a salary and television audience.

Producers were beginning to take notice of us, and there was talk that BeBe and I would be doing an album together. I knew that God was using BeBe and me at *PTL*, and the hundreds of letters and phone calls that came in every week complimenting our work were confirmation of that. More and more invitations to sing together were pouring in. Despite some awkwardness in the beginning, BeBe and I were beginning to enjoy singing together. We had been singing together long enough now to know each other's style. We knew each other's pace, we knew each other's strengths and weaknesses, and we knew how to draw on each other's strength and how to compensate for the other's weaknesses. Best of all, we were family. As family, we trusted each other and were comfortable with each other. This was the important part. We knew singers who were greater than we were, but it takes more than a great voice to sing. It takes being comfortable and relaxed enough with who you are, with your setting, and with those around you to sing a song and make music.

❦ ❦

With my brother by my side, I wasn't out there alone. As early as my days at *PTL*, I was discovering that performing can be a crazy, cutthroat business. With BeBe as my copartner, I knew I had someone who was in my corner and someone who shared my vision of singing as a ministry, and he knew he had the same in me. It was good to have someone around I could cut a knowing eye over at when things got bizarre. Sometimes we could communicate just by looking at each other. Like the time we had to dress up in cowboy and cowgirl clothes for a particular show on the telecast. I was embarrassed. We put on our wardrobes in a fit of giggles. "Lord, if they could see us back at Shalom Temple, we'd be laughed out of the church," BeBe said with cowboy rope in his hand. "You look like a black Roy Rogers," I teased.

"You look like Trigger," BeBe shot back.

"Remind me to pray for you, boy," I said laughing.

Knowing that I could expect a phone call from Alvin at night gave me something to look forward to when I came home tired and exhausted. Besides the fact that he made me feel safe, part of what I liked about Alvin was that he wasn't in the business. He reminded me that there were things to talk about other than music and singing. Alvin was a business-man. I liked having someone in my life whose first question to me was not "What song are you working on?" Knowing that at eleven that night someone would be on the other end of the line asking, "How is CeCe doing?" was heartwarming. Alvin brought a totally different perspective and conversation into my life. During my three years at *PTL*, almost everyone I met was involved in some aspect of music. It was refreshing to be with someone who cared about CeCe, or better yet, someone who cared about Priscilla the woman, the little brown girl with the shy demeanor. He worried about me and called to check that I was eating right, sleeping right, and getting my rest. As the oldest girl in my family, it was my role to do that for everyone else. I was always playing Mom with BeBe, reminding him of things I knew he'd forget, reprimanding him about his choices, telling him what he ought to be doing. I knew he resented me for it sometimes.

But, finally, someone was fussing over me—someone who wasn't related to *me*. Alvin didn't care that I sang with *PTL* ministries, that I sang on television everyday, or that BeBe and I had traveled to Portugal a year earlier to sing at a big Christian gathering. He was proud of my work, but he would have loved me if I was the hairstylist I'd gone to school to become. When I told him about the trip to Portugal, his only response was, "I bet you were homesick the whole time." He was right—I was.

Eventually I grew restless at *PTL*. I began feeling disconnected to the flurry of activities that went with the job. I began feeling that it was time to go. Unsure where I would go or what I would do if I left, I knew it was time for a different pace. Of course, everyone thought Alvin was the exclusive reason for my eventual departure, but he wasn't. I was ready to go. It was time, God's time. The truth is that I had never stopped missing home. I knew that BeBe missed home as well, but he wasn't as ready as I was to return. He was busy trying his hand at other things, like meeting producers, and becoming more familiar with the business end of music; most important, he was beginning to get excited about writing and arranging songs. I was happy for him, but I was restless. I could see that somewhere in the process of living out my years in Charlotte, I'd lost something along the way. I loved my work, my ministry at *PTL* and my travels around the country singing were thriving, but a part of me was desperately lonely. BeBe had his life, Howard and Shay, our friends, had each other, Penny was always off somewhere swept up in her own hilarious drama, but part of me felt unglued. I had my Mom and my Dad, and my sisters and brothers back home, but I needed more. I wanted to know what it felt like to give myself over to something else, something other than career, church, religion, parents, siblings. I needed to feel connected to something— and someone— that didn't have to do with the business I was in. I needed to go home. I needed a different kind of home. I needed somewhere and someone that made me feel grounded. What I knew was that love and loving Alvin made me feel courageous enough to try something new. Sometimes being afraid and clinging to what you know is familiar is more painful than risking love and the chance to grow. I was ready to take that risk.

Love

Love is a wonderful thing,
You recognize it right away.
Your heart starts to sing,
And you wear a smile all day.
It's a fresh light feeling.
Nothing else can compare;
Love always gives,
Love always cares.

It was here from the beginning,
And will be here at the end;
Love is the greatest gift of all,
Love always wins.

9

Family First

Let all things be done decently
and in order.
—1 Cor. 14:40

I left *PTL* for the chance to
grow, and love is one of the best ways to make you grow. For
one thing, love forces you constantly to make choices. Love is
a choice. When I left in the spring of 1984 I chose to love
Alvin, and to keep growing. Once I finally made the decision
to jump off the cliff and to learn to get accustomed to the feel
of falling, I knew I could do anything—including walk away
from my so-called glamorous job at *PTL*. I had learned
everything God had sent me there to learn, and it was time to
move on.

Unfortunately, all my family did not see things exactly the same way. Everyone knew that Alvin and I were seeing each other, and had been doing so for over a year, flying back and forth between Detroit and Charlotte when we could, amassing large phone bills, writing letters, trying to stay in touch. I had been talking all along to my parents about Alvin and the possibility of marrying him. It was no surprise to them, then, when we decided finally to seal our relationship. Mom knew that her daughter had grown up to become a woman. She noticed the changes in me each time I came home: the makeup, the earrings, the air of confidence. She knew her little girl was in love, even though I was only nineteen going on twenty. She recognized the signs of an almost twenty-year-old girl falling in love. She had once been eighteen and madly in love with my father. "Baby, have you prayed about it?" she asked me one night when I called her from Charlotte.

"Yes, Mom."

"Are you sure about it?" she asked with motherly concern.

"Yes, Mom, I'm sure about it," I answered her, never more sure about anything in my life.

I heard her sigh with relief. "If the Lord is in it, everything will be all right," she answered in that soft, comforting voice of hers. My father would ask me the same question later, and then bow his head and ask God to bless me and take care of me when I gave him my answer. Tears welled in my eyes as I listened to him pray for me. He asked God to make His will clear, for like any father he wanted his daughter to experience with the man she loved even more love and joy than he and Mom had known in their long marriage.

I decided I wouldn't marry Alvin until my parents and elders had peace about it. I wanted instructions from my pastor, and I needed the blessing of my entire family. I went to my pastor, Elder Stacks, and asked him to join me in prayer. Elder Stacks counseled me constantly those early months of my engagement to Alvin. One day I saw Elder Stacks at church during a friend's wedding. He pulled me aside in the corridor and said, "I have something to tell you." A feeling of dread ran through me. I just knew he was going to say that Alvin wasn't the one for me. "Alvin is a man of God," Elder Stacks began to say. "Alvin loves God, he's faithful, and he's a jewel." That was the confirmation my heart needed. Elder Stacks had been my pastor since I was a little girl. In 1966 just after my grandfather died he took over the church my grandfather had founded. Although my parents loved Alvin, and never tried to persuade me one way or another, I was still praying for their hearty approval. That was very important to me, because I respected them so much. God made me wait and give them the time they needed. I knew that if anyone could give them peace about my decision, God could. God could speak to them just as God had spoken to me.

My brothers, however, who always thought of themselves as my protectors, were less serene about the matter. I was the first girl in the family to get married. As was to be expected, my brothers were downright protective and suspicious, as brothers should be. I don't think they meant any harm, they had nothing personal against Alvin, but their little sister was talking about getting married. Theirs were the typical complaints of brothers who'd never had to share their sister's affections with another man. "What do you see in him?" asked one of them. "He doesn't sing, act, play an instrument, or anything!" He was concerned that marriage was only going to hinder my career. Marvin, who had been married several years already said that I had to love Alvin enough to give up everything. And I did. I stood my ground with them. When they saw that my mind was made up, each brother relented—*slowly, eventually, and some begrudgingly.* Ronald, the brother who'd taught me how to color my dolls' hair, was the last one to come around. It was uncertain until the final day whether he was even going to show up for the wedding. But he did, like I knew he would— because his love for his sister was greater than his doubts about her decision to marry and jeopardize her career. Like my mother, I can appear calm and laid back, but also like my mother, I can dig my heels in when I've made up my mind and stand up for my beliefs. I believed God had brought Alvin and me together. Loving Alvin Love was right.

Leaving my job singing at *PTL* and returning to marry Alvin was the right decision for me. Even though I didn't know what I was going to do back in Detroit, even though I didn't know what was next, I kept assuring my family, "I've left *PTL*, but I haven't stopped singing," which was completely true. I believed that if God wanted me to keep singing, He would make a way for me to keep singing. I still looked forward to singing with BeBe—we were joined at the hip now. BeBe had decided to remain for a while in Charlotte with *PTL*, but he was branching out into writing music. We made an independent album with *PTL* called *Lord Lift Us Up,* which came out about the time I was returning to Detroit. We completed the album in three days, and BeBe and I didn't even see the producers the whole time we were recording. They were upstairs in a booth. We could hear them on the earphones, but we never saw them the whole time. The album capitalized on our popularity on the *PTL Show* and was a successful. Judging by the way BeBe's phone continued to ring off the hook down in Charlotte, there was still plenty of interest in booking us, despite my leaving *PTL*. There were always invitations coming in for us to sing at some church or concert hall. I agreed to fly straight to the city where we had to sing and meet him there. Gospel had come a long way from the days of quartet singers who were forced to drive from state to state to get to their gigs.

When I moved back to Detroit from Charlotte and moved back in with my parents, they got the chance to see

Alvin and me together and to see the way Alvin and I looked at each other when we were together. They had to relent when they saw the mirror image of their own love as it had begun almost thirty-four years before.

On June 23, 1984, I became Mrs. Alvin Love. Marvin's wife, Vicki, helped to organize the wedding and had the church decorated with beautiful pink and fuschia flowers. It was a gorgeous wedding, every girl's dream. My father looked dapper and handsome in his tuxedo as he escorted me down the aisle. I'll never forget what he said to comfort me as we made that long walk down the middle of the church: "Don't be nervous, baby, just act like it's another concert." I suspect that the hardest words my father ever uttered were "I do" when Elder Stack posed the question, "Who gives this woman?" I was his daughter, his first girl. He never meant to give me away. He was just walking his daughter down the aisle. Although racked by their own emotions, my brothers joined BeBe in a song he had written, "I'm Going to Miss You," to mark the occasion when their sister ceased to be *just* their sister. Dapper in his suit, the spitting image of my father, BeBe was very handsome. I was determined not to cry at the sight of them singing and letting me go. I didn't want makeup to run down my face. I was moved with a sister's love and appreciation.

Because he was a man and not a boy, Alvin understood that when he married me he had married my whole rambunctious family, but he was undeterred. When he looked into my eyes, his eyes told me everything I needed to know: our love was for the long haul. Erect and calm, he slipped the ring on my finger and pledged to love me for the rest of his life, for richer and poorer, through good times and bad, in sickness and in health. Whoever first wrote those words centuries ago was not just a poet, he was someone obviously who had experienced the excruciating highs and lows of love and was familiar with the winepress of intimacy. Behind a veil of smiles, I pledged to Alvin to do the same.

Being called "Sister Love" took some getting used to. Every time someone from church greeted me as Sister Love, I thought they were referring to someone else. Sister Love had a playful but affectionate ring to it. Not only did it take some getting used to but it also took some time to combine my two new identities—as CeCe Winans the singer (I had accepted the fact that I was a singer now) and Mrs. Alvin Love, the wife. Any trouble I had was in my own head. Alvin never asked me to stop being CeCe Winans. He wanted me to continue singing. Sometimes he had to make me get on a plane to go sing. Producers and records companies were interested in talking with BeBe and me about recording. He had written his beautiful ballad "I'm Going to Miss You" as though I was gone from him and the business for good. But when he saw that we would continue to sing as a duet, he stopped pacing the floor and continued to write music for us to record.

Meanwhile I threw all my energies in the beginning into being wife, friend, confidante, prayer partner, and lover to Alvin Love. Because I had never finished cosmetology school and hate starting things and not finishing them, I reenrolled in Virginia Farrell Cosmetology School and got my beautician's license. Soon after I finished school I opened up a shop on Livernois and called it "CeCe's." Opening the shop was a great backup plan, although it demanded a lot of hard work. I insisted upon having a job on the side, a source of steady income, just in case singing independently yielded unsteady income. I didn't believe in putting all my eggs in one basket.

I was determined not to get stuck and be poor, and I knew how unpredictable the music and entertainment business could be. I'd had enough chances to hear the hard-luck stories of singers who had come on the *PTL* broadcast. Besides the all-too-usual tales of record companies and managers cheating singers out of millions of dollars of royalties, there was the fact that audience's tastes change from year to year. One minute you're a hit, the next minute you're out. I didn't want that to happen to me. Owning my own beauty shop gave me the flexibility I needed. It also ensured that I would never again have to stand in line and wait for a hair appointment. I would find out later that for years Mahalia Jackson owned and operated a beauty salon there in Chicago where she lived. In the beginning years of her career, she stood on her feet fixing hair during the week and then stood on her feet and sang before packed churches on the weekend.

My business expanded to fourteen operators renting chairs in my shop. Every day was a soap opera. Someone didn't come to work, someone else was having man troubles and couldn't keep her mind on her work, someone was stealing someone else's supplies, someone messed up a client's head and the client was threatening to sue. I had Alvin and my father to thank for watching out at the shop for me. They managed and ran things, dividing the tasks between them when things became too much for me. It was clear that owning a beauty shop was about more than fixing hair. It was about taking care of a business. I had to learn the business side of hair care very quickly. Hiring and firing operators was very hard for someone with my laid-back personality. I was always trying to find a way to make things work. But eventually I had to toughen up and learned the hard lessons of being an entrepreneur. Learning the delicate art of hiring and firing people who worked for me would come in handy years later when as an artist I had to summon the courage to hire and fire managers, lawyers, and band members.

I hardly had time to be around by the time the shop expanded and grew to fourteen operators. For one thing, I was pregnant after only a year of being married. I had been complaining about feeling always weak and sluggish and could barely stand on my feet at the shop or tolerate the high altitudes of being in a plane. I thought I had caught something.

Leave it to Grandmother Howze before she died to diagnose the matter succinctly: "You probably got that nine-month virus that's going around." Exhaustion robbed me of any appreciation of subtleties. I didn't catch her drift at first. She was right. Nine months later, on June 20, 1985, I gave birth to a seven-pound-four-ounce bouncing baby boy, Alvin Lemar Love III.

There are no private moments when you have a big family. Every event is a family affair. The night I went into labor with my son, we had a labor party there at our home on Whitcomb Street. Mom, Dad, my brothers and sisters all gathered at our house, laughing, teasing, and carousing both to celebrate the pending birth of the baby by the oldest girl in the family and to help take my mind off the labor pains. When the pains became too much, Alvin took me to the hospital, only to find out that the labor pains were false. I hadn't even dilated. As we started on our way out of the hospital, a nurse, seeing our disappointment, recommended that I sip a bit of wine if I wanted to hurry the delivery along. If the pains were false, wine would make them go away, she counseled. But if the pains were the real thing, the wine would hurry things along. By then I was tired and exhausted and frustrated enough to take her on. I was miserable too, having gained some fifty pounds with this pregnancy. Alvin stopped off at a liquor store on the way home and went in to buy some wine. After only a few seconds inside he came out to the car with a sheepish look on his face and asked, "White wine or red wine?" "I don't know!" I yelled, feeling uncomfortable from both being so pregnant and sitting in a car outside a liquor store. I didn't know a thing about buying wine! He came back with red wine, and after gulping a glass down once we got home, within a few hours the contractions started coming hard and fast. No more cute false labor, this was the *real* thing. Rushing back to the Beaumont Hospital, it seemed that Alvin drove our little Honda over every bump in the road. I fussed and moaned the entire ride. The family was at the hospital when I got there, but this time, the party was over. The contractions were coming very quickly now. Mom, poor thing, could not stay in the room with me. She had given birth to ten children of her own, but she nearly fainted because she just couldn't bear to watch her oldest daughter suffer with her own labor pains.

I'm proud of the fact that I saw our decision for a natural birth through, but for a while there it was touch and go: Alvin pumping me with ice chips between contractions, and me moaning and crying during every contraction. There was one moment when I completely lost it and almost begged for an epidural. That was when the nurse came in to check my contractions and announced that I still had a while to go, since I had dilated only a few centimeters. I rebuked that comment. No way could I endure an interminable more amount of time in labor. A short while later, a couple of hours to be exact, my beautiful son was on his way into the world. I heard Alvin yelling, "CeCe, it's coming. CeCe it's coming!"

When the nurses put my son in my arms I couldn't bear to let him go. I'd never loved anyone so instantly and so powerfully before in my life. I hadn't even fallen in love with his father that way. Our love had grown out of our friendship. But it would be just the opposite with the dark handsome bundle I now held in my arms. I loved him first and then would get to know him as a special little friend in my life. It felt as though I had already lived a thousand lifetimes, and now I had earned the right to be a mother. I was just twenty years old, too young to be a mother, some might say, but I didn't think so when I considered how much love there was in my life and family to go around.

❧ ❧

BeBe and I signed with Sparrow Records later that year and then we recorded a single with Sparrow that did spectacularly well on the charts, "I. O. U. Me." The day we signed on the dotted line with Sparrow we were beside ourselves with joy. Finally, we were bona fide recording artists. I was a singer, a *real* singer, with a contract and a manager to prove it. I had a headache to prove it. I went home to celebrate with Alvin and Little Alvin. My husband was overjoyed. Little Alvin was equally overjoyed. He giggled and gurgled and threw up milk all over the bed covers.

When you first hear yourself on the radio, it's weird. At first, you don't even recognize that it's you singing. It's your voice, it's your song, but it's not you. It's like standing outside yourself listening to yourself, filled with sheer disbelief. I had always dogged BeBe about his songwriting. I teased him mercilessly, in good old Winans fashion. "You know you can't write." "You can't even spell." "Nobody is going to want to hear that stuff." The first time we heard BeBe's song "I.O.U. Me" the two of us were riding in a car. BeBe had moved back to Detroit. "BeBe! BeBe! BeBe!" I screamed. "That's you! That's me. That's us! That's your song!" BeBe sat in the seat in stunned silence. "I can't believe they're playing your song!" I yelled. "I can't believe I'm singing your song!" I teased. We laughed and turned the volume up as high as it would go. I was so proud of my brother I could burst. My brother was a songwriter.

Many of the songs on our debut album were written and produced by BeBe and producer (and friend) Keith Thomas. The two of them created the BeBe & CeCe sound. BeBe's lyrics and background vocals arrangements combined with Keith's hit-making genius for pop music combined to successfully arrive at a sound that was contemporary, hip, smooth, and striking. Compared with the three days BeBe and I had spent in the studio years earlier recording the *PTL* album, months went into making this album. They wouldn't release it until they were sure the sound coming out of the speakers was the same as what they were hearing in their heads. Motherhood restricted the amount of time I could give to flying back and forth to Nashville for recording sessions. With my second pregnancy I was about to understand how my mother felt when twenty-two years earlier she had propped herself up on her arms on the delivery table, and upon hearing that I was born, asked the doctor three times, "Did you say it's a girl?" I was pregnant with our daughter, Ashley Rose, when our debut album, *Introducing BeBe & CeCe Winans*, came out. My mother was concerned that the excitement from all the publicity and travel associated with a new release would send me into an early delivery—or worse. I wasn't able to travel as much with my second pregnancy as I had with my first pregnancy. Not only were there more physical complications carrying my daughter, but I doubt there was a safety belt made that would have reached over my enormous front part. *Introducing* went on to sell over 300,000 copies and featured two singles that were number one on the Christian radio, "I.O.U. Me" and "For Always." I delivered my baby girl on September 5, 1987. Ashley was the most beautiful child in the nursery. Her mother and father, grandparents, and uncles and aunts agreed. This time, Mom's face was the first face I saw when my eyes opened.

"How did you do it, Mom, giving birth to ten children?" I asked her groggily.

"The question is: how did *you* do it?" she asked, bursting with pride.

"Do what?" I asked.

"How did you manage to have a girl on just your second try?" We both laughed.

❦ ❦

I am often asked "What is success?" To me success is when you don't have to worry about it happening. You can put your efforts into doing what you like, what you're good at, what you're called to do. God does the rest. That to me is success. I have been successful in this business in that I never sat down and planned the things that have happened to me. I could never have imagined for myself becoming a professional singer. Who could have imagined that two releases from our first album, "I.O.U. Me" and "For Always," would become best-sellers on both the R & B and the Inspirational charts? And to be voted as a duo "Best New Artists" in the 1987 Dove Awards afterward, and me a Grammy for "Best Soul Gospel Performance, Female" for "For Always"—it was all inconceivable! We were beside ourselves when the news came in that we'd been nominated. We called the whole family, and everyone laughed and shouted with us. You imagine what you would say for your acceptance speech if you ever won a Grammy, but that first time all that came to mind is: "Thank you, Jesus!"

After that first album the phone calls started coming, the guest appearances, the interviews, the offers, and the contracts started coming in. I was reeling. It was a heady experience. Then there were awards from our peers confirming that we had arrived. We had to learn how to handle success. I learned what I learned through trial and error, through good advice, through studying other people's example. I learned that you have to take care of business. You can't depend on anyone to protect you from anything. God wants us to be excellent in everything we do and that includes business. God will help you, but you must do your part by being prepared. For instance, during those first few years even with Grammy nominations and eventually Stella awards under our belt we found that we were still vulnerable to being ripped off. We were young and naive in those early years. We performed in Philadelphia once, and the promoter took off before we were paid. We were left out on the street, outside the auditorium, in the pouring rain with all our luggage on the sidewalk. My mother, who had flown up from Detroit to be with us, was out on the street in the rain with us. It was a mess. Thank heaven there is a merciful God who saw to it that our friends Tramaine Hawkins and her manager, Buster Soaries, were riding down the streets of Philadelphia at just the right moment. Tramaine had appeared on the same program with us, but being more experienced in the business than we were, she had been paid. "Is that CeCe and BeBe?" Tramaine asked her manager, peering out the window. They stopped the car, picked us up, and took us out to dinner. We were wet, cold, hungry, and they took us in. There were many times like this when we trusted promoters, managers, producers, and found ourselves in the end ripped off. There were a number of times when poor BeBe had to fork up money to cover all our expenses, including paying for return airline tickets home for him, me, and the whole band on his credit card. Eventually, you learn to set your priorities. Get ripped off enough times and you learn to ask for round-trip airline tickets and half of your money up front.

I used to avoid making decisions. I didn't want to do it and left it up to BeBe. I would do everything to avoid it. I left it to him to hire and fire backup people. For years there, our younger sisters, Angie, Debbie, and our sister-in-law Regina were the only people we would hire to do backup. It was hard to find reliable people to hire. It was harder to fire the sorry people you'd hired. Since then I've had to learn how to be a businesswoman. I've had to learn to be tougher. You learn to trust God to help you do what He has called you to do. I am convinced that I wouldn't want to be in this business without God. It is hard work with God; it's crushing without God.

❧ ❧

Of all the awards I would receive over the next decade of my career—the seven Grammys, seven Gospel Music

Association Dove Awards, three NAACP Image Awards, the platinum and gold records— none would compare with the reward of being a mother and wife. Being a wife and mother at such a young age meant that I would have to juggle marriage, mothering, and singing for as long as I would be making records. For a while there, before and after Ashley was born, I cut down on the travel. All I wanted was to be home with my babies and husband.

I could never have managed all these years without Alvin. He has never wavered in his support. There were many times when I anguished over having to leave home to go sing, and Alvin would be the one to say, "Stop crying, and go do what the Lord has for you to do." He has proven to be a loving father and husband. We've grown together, and we've learned to do what we've needed to keep this marriage, family, and this music career going. To this day I don't know how my parents did it with ten children.

The only ways that I know of to help raise a family are to prioritize and sacrifice. There have been a lot of parties that I missed out on trying to get back home to the family I love. I had PTA meetings, recitals, and doctor appointments to get back to. Somebody back home was waiting for me and looking for me. I needed them. I learned that eventually the music stops and the party ends, and you discover that only love is real.

Priorities

Priorities must be set in order to keep things in line;
eliminate confusion and peace you will find.
When God is the head of your life,
everything else falls into place;
Family comes first
because you need their warm embrace.
Life is full of changes,
so changes have to be made.
Priorities are most important;
they keep you balanced and focused so never let them
    fade.

10

Follow the Spirit

There is therefore no condemnation
to those who are in Jesus Christ,
who walk not after the flesh,
but after the spirit.
—*Rom. 8:1*

Oprah Winfrey once asked us during a guest appearance as a family on her show whether we were willing to admit to any competition among us as siblings, since almost all of us were professional singers. Marvin answered with a sly grin, "Let's say it like this: you don't want to be the one in any given year who has the worst album in the Winans family." My husband, Alvin, concurs: "Although I've never seen a family that enjoys each other so much, the Winans are one of the most competitive families I've ever met in my life." Both Marvin and Alvin are right. The Winans take their music seriously, and we always have. From as far back as the time when the whole family sat around the old upright piano in Mom and Dad's living room in Detroit—taking turns singing harmonies, dividing ourselves up into groups and singing parts, singing lead, singing solos—there has always been a healthy amount of jostling and razzing among us about our singing. But the jostling and razzing has never been about who sings the best. It's more like who sings *the worst.* "Ah, man, you can't sing." "You call that singing?" "When you *start* singing, please let me know." Mom and Dad were blessed to have ten children who sing, but in a family of ten singing children, there is bound to be a healthy amount of teasing going on about who sings the worst. We were hard on one another as kids, and we've been hard on one another as we've grown up and branched out into our different musical careers.

The truth is that our jibes and pokes at one another have never been about competition, never about being the best singer in the family. It's about pacing one another toward excellence in our ministries as artists. We are a competitive family in the best sense of the word. Whether it was at home or in our family concerts or at church, we've always had competitive situations that inspired us to do better and to do our best, but the competition never centered around tearing one another down so as to make another look good. When our *Heaven* album was the first album to go gold, our brothers The Winans said, "Well, we'll just have to come on strong with our next recording." So we said, "Don't come out with an album that does *not* go gold," and their next album did go gold! Then our album *Lifestyles* went platinum, which really gave them a run for their money. When *Lifestyles* went platinum, no one was happier than my brothers and sisters. "Together we stand, divided we fall," Dad has always reminded us.

Teasing and joking go hand in hand with growing up in a big family. You develop a thick skin to all the teasing that goes back and forth or you walk around with your feelings bruised all the time, but it's all done in love. Many times over the years our ability to laugh at each other and at ourselves has been just the pressure release that BeBe and I needed to get through rehearsals, hard times, and performances.

One advantage of so much teasing is that we were never allowed to take ourselves too seriously. We see to it that no one thinks too much of himself or herself. We keep one another's feet firmly planted on the earth. Over the years we've called one another back and forth or left messages on the telephone after seeing one another on the television or after the release of a CD: "Lord, who wrote that song?" or "Who told you to wear that on television?" or "Your hairstyle was not the right one; use another makeup artist" or "You looked like a clown." You learn to give as good as you get. As brothers and sisters we have been hard on one another in our teasing. But we're also the first to support one another and to praise one another. We learned that from our parents. When The Winans received their first Grammy in 1983 for "Best Soul Gospel," the whole family cheered, celebrated, cried, and thanked God. BeBe and I were right there, showering our brothers with hugs and kisses. Likewise when our first album garnered for us the GMA Best New Artist award in 1988, as well as a Grammy award for "For Always," no one celebrated more than our brothers The Winans as well as the entire Winans clan.

Thank God, I have come a long way since the days when my brothers' teasing and jokes reduced me to tears. Now I can give as well as I can take. "Uh, uh . . . just where do you think you're going in that wig," BeBe turned to say to me many times just before we were to go out and perform. "You just concentrate on singing, and not on my hair, so I won't outsing you and blow you off the stage!" I would say under my breath between songs. The object was to try to keep straight faces as we poked fun at each other, which in the black community is called "playing the dozens." Unfortunately, I usually lost the bargain. I could never keep a straight face and would have to break out with a big grin during a song. It doesn't take much to make me laugh. I'm glad I learned to laugh at myself because later on, with a husband and children, the razzing never stopped. "Mom," Alvin Jr. would say to me the next

morning around the breakfast table after watching me perform the night before, "you sang too long last night, and your
voice was all off!" "Yeah, Mom," Ashley might chime in, "be
sure never to make that face again when you say, 'Hallelujah.'"

"Thanks guys," I exclaim, forking over their eggs onto
their plates, my hair all over my head, sleep in the corner of my
eyes, with my favorite old nightshirt on. "By the way, why did
you let them fix your hair like that?" my husband will add with
his own sly, handsome grin looking up over some papers.
Nothing like a family to help keep you from believing your own
press! If I didn't know that my family loved me, I would always
be in tears. As it is, I take a deep breath and take my knocks, and
when it's my turn to tease, I pay them back.

People frequently ask how our family has survived all the
teasing. The answer is simple: we have never doubted one
another's love.

It's a good thing that there were so many siblings in my
family and that we learned to endure one another's razzing
and teasing over the years because otherwise we might have
been devastated by the comments of our critics. Despite the
numerous awards our music has garnered, not all the critics
have been taken with our brand of inspirational songs. Some
of the criticism has been downright harsh and cruel, and I
would be less than honest if I said that it hasn't hurt. Many
have criticized the contemporary urban sound and tone of our
music as not constituting authentic gospel music. It was naive

of us, but when we started singing we anticipated the enthusiastic support of the church. We thought the church would be happy that we were spreading the gospel message with a sound with which youth could identify, but we were wrong. We have been accused of selling out gospel, of not being Christian enough, of not loving God, and of just being after the money. Those were really hard. Some of our worst criticism has come from those in the church.

All we have ever wanted to do was to sing songs that were in our hearts, songs that ministered to and encouraged people, and songs that glorified the power and presence of the Lord. For years gospel was done one way, and it was missing a lot of people. I love the traditional songs. I grew up singing great hymns like "Amazing Grace," and "Great Is Thy Faithfulness." But I know that everyone doesn't have the religious background that I have had. So as products of our generation we have created sounds that catch younger people who might otherwise never hear about the Lord or never hear positive lyrics. We were two kids who grew up on the contemporary happening gospel sounds of Andrae Crouch, Walter and Edwin Hawkins, and Rance Allen, who loved God and did the music we loved. Contemporary music was nothing new for us.

ॐॐ

In the beginning, the criticism made me second-guess myself sometimes and want to apologize for our music. I was always looking over my shoulder and bracing myself for the worst after each recording, but fortunately, BeBe had thicker skin. He was always the go-getter. He never admitted it, but I know there were times when the reviews hurt. Thank God he never stopped writing. Songs like our 1991 "Addictive Love" or the remake of the Staple Singers' song "I'll Take You There" might never have gotten sung if we had allowed ourselves to be paralyzed by the criticism. Both songs charged to the top of R & B single charts as well as national Christian radio charts. Evidently audiences, both the Christian and secular, have disagreed with the critics and found our message of hope captivating and inspirational. It's music from the heart, and I think that's why it goes straight to the hearts of others. That both songs achieved platinum status and topped the charts helped to confirm for us that our music was reaching people just as God intended. I think about all the criticism we have endured over the years, those who want to draw a sharp line between different kinds of music, and then I remember the tears and faces of the young people at Mercy College during our family concerts years ago and the handshakes and kisses of those we've encountered in our travel over the years who have said that they came back to the church and the Lord because they had our music in their lives.

For a long time we didn't fully understand the positive results of our crossover music until the letters and calls started coming in. People would say that they were on the dance floor, dancing to this or that song, but the lyrics kept lingering in their heads. They found themselves drawn to return to church afterward. Some were able to accept Christ, and turned their lives around. It takes all kinds of different music to reach the vast numbers of different kinds of people. I learned that at some point, when you believe God has called you to do something, forget about what people say. Seek God's favor first, and everything else will fall into place.

One day, however, I forgot my own lesson. When I met the singers from the gospel group called Gospel Gangsta and I immediately judged them because of the name of their group, I had forgotten my advice, but the voice of the Lord convicted me in my heart on the spot: *you're judging them before you give them a chance.* So when they asked me after a meeting to come hear them at a Christian club later that night I relented. Their kind, gentle manner won me over and convinced me to go. After all, I was curious. God totally changed my critical attitude! These men, who were saved from a life of gangs, guns, and death, are reaching out to gang members with power and love—talking to them about sex, drugs, and violence, and offering hope to those who have run out of hope. That night was a powerful example of what "coming together" means. I was able to understand somebody else's call because God prodded me, first to step past my own preconceived attitudes, and then to see how God uses our unique talents and backgrounds. There were some in the audience who probably could never relate to what may seem like the clean, upbeat, violin sounds in the background of BeBe & CeCe, but they could identify with the rapping, funky, streetwise rhythms of Gospel Gangsta. And there are those who prefer the down-home, rousing traditional gospel roots of the first lady of gospel, Shirley Caesar, over either BeBe & CeCe or Gospel Gangsta. As long as God's name is praised and people's hearts are encouraged, we should stop judging whose music is best, preferable, authentic, or really Christian, myself included.

The most important thing in this industry is finding your own place and learning to be yourself: finding out exactly what God has called you to do and doing it. When you're in this business, you're tempted to try on and take off a thousand masks, especially if you're female. Looking back over some of the outfits I've donned, the hairstyles I've worn, the musical styles I've tried that weren't me but that I tried anyway because someone told me to do, or because I was trying to conform to other people's image of what I should be—I am angry at myself for all that wasted energy and time! Some costly mistakes were made because I didn't trust myself enough to follow my own heart.

Take, for example, the ghastly mistake BeBe and I made signing our first management agreement. To this day BeBe and I tease each other that it was the other's fault. But the truth is that we were both young and stupid and didn't listen to our hearts.

This first manager was recommended to us by someone else in the industry whom we trusted. We had just released our first album, *Introducing*, and we were doing a lot of traveling and giving a lot of interviews. Things were moving pretty fast. The prospect of hiring someone to manage all the chaos and craziness that comes with being recording artists was exciting. We flew to New York to meet our prospective manager in his office, and, boy, were we impressed. Pictures of him with other well-established artists he'd managed were all over his office. It never dawned on us to ask whether any of these artists in the pictures were happy or pleased with his management. He began telling us all the stuff he could do for us: the engagements he could get for us, the money he could negotiate for us, the deals he could secure for us. We were so young, eager, and grateful. When you're a kid, you just want to use your talent, you just want to sing, but you don't know that singing is a business. So you start out trusting everybody. But in the meanwhile, they are mismanaging you. To this day, BeBe and I are still mad at ourselves for not asking the questions we should have. It was a lesson in learning to listen to your own conscience. We thought we needed this manager, and it never dawned on us that we were the ones doing all the work. The relationship should exist as a result of the artists and not the agents.

All the time while the guy was talking, I was feeling uncomfortable. Something felt strange, and my spirit couldn't relax. I thought I was just nervous, but that wasn't it at all. All of a sudden I started crying in the man's office—I couldn't help myself. BeBe was sitting next to me giving me this look that said "Don't fall apart on me now." I liked the man, but something in me kept telling me not to sign the contract he was pushing in our faces. I couldn't figure out why I shouldn't do it. He's talking, BeBe's talking, I'm listening . . . and I'm crying.

When the time came to sign, I was signing and weeping at the same time. It all looked good and sounded good, but it ended up being one of our biggest mistakes. Within just a few months it was obvious that we'd made a mistake. We realized that we'd signed on with someone we felt was not looking out for our best interests. We did all the work, but we were paying someone who got his money right off the top for few or no services. We later learned that there is no such thing as a standard contract. In fact the country singer Kenny Rogers was the one who told me years later that he has had the same manager for more than twenty-five years with nothing more than a handshake and their word as their contract. "As an artist, you decide the terms of the contract," he told me. If BeBe and I had sought advice from others in the industry, we might have avoided those first mistakes. But we spent all our time those first years singing and not learning the business side of this work.

We were kids who were excited and who got stuck for five years with a man we liked as a person but not as a manager. He was a manager and a lawyer, and the deal was done. Fortunately, through it all, the Lord watched over us. It's true that "the Lord watches over babies and those who do foolish things." And BeBe and I were both. But God knew our hearts, and because BeBe and I were honorable people and didn't try to cheat him, God still opened doors, on the principle, I believe, that we saw our contract through. At first, BeBe and I were angry and didn't want to hold up the contract, but we knew that it was our own mistake. We signed willingly, though foolishly, and because we saw it through honorably, God gave us favor throughout the entertainment industry. Our careers took off during those first five years at a pace that we could not even have imagined—no thanks to our manager, but all praises due to God. Instead, God taught us a few choice lessons. First, look, pray, seek counsel before signing contracts. Second, to paraphrase a verse from the Bible, "'Your success is not by your power, nor by your strength *nor by the wheeling and dealing of managers*, but by my Spirit,' says the Lord."

To this day, I am allergic to contracts. Start talking to me about contracts, and I start scratching . . . but then I start reading the fine print. I didn't speak up back then because I didn't want to look green. I didn't want to look as if I didn't know what I was doing—and I didn't. Five years is a long time, but it could have been longer, however. It could have been a more complicated contract that extended into all areas of my life.

A lot of black artists die poor because they didn't take care of their business. I would love someday to set up an organization of some sort that would counsel young artists on how to take care of their business. All you want to do in the beginning is to sing. You forget that there's a business side to the art.

Fifteen years later BeBe still teases me, saying, "Girl, I don't know why *you* signed that contract." And I cut my eyes over at him and say,"Oh yeah, right." The simple truth is we both were intimidated. We should have stalled for time. Being just a young black woman, I doubted my intelligence. What do I know? I asked myself. I should have asked for time to think about it. Outnumbered by men—my brother and the smooth-talking male manager—I was too scared to speak up. Trust your gut, I eventually learned. It's probably God speaking. I also learned that if I don't feel like signing it today, if it's the right thing for me, tomorrow will be fine. Timing is important. You don't always have to go when people tell you to go. I should have sought God through prayer and fasting. But I didn't. Looking back on it, I say to myself, "Oh wow, God was in my tears as I sat there crying in the office, and I didn't pay Him any attention."

Eventually you learn to trust your instincts, your own style, and most of all, your anointing. You learn to be true to yourself. "Just be yourself," Mom and Dad cautioned me over the years. "Just be yourself."

They were so right. Nobody can beat you at being you.

New people will always come along who sing better than you, look better than you, project better than you, but nobody can beat you at being *you*. Follow God, follow your heart, and be yourself, and you're bound to find God there on your path waiting for you. Not only will God be there waiting, but God will give you new opportunities and new friends. This business of performing has a way of driving wedges in relationships, stirring up jealousy in people, and reducing people to clawing at one another in competitive situations rather than pacing one another toward excellence.

If I'd listened to others instead of to my own heart, I would never have met my dear friend, superstar Whitney Houston.

∾ ∾

The playwright Lorraine Hansberry once wrote, "The thing that makes you exceptional is also that which makes you lonely." Growing up in a large family afforded me the luxury of never having to go outside of family for companionship and friendship, but one day I grew up and was blessed to have friendships beyond the narrow cocoon of my family. I was blessed to find that friendship in Whitney Houston. We met at the NAACP Image Awards ceremony around 1988 out in Los Angeles. After blowing me away with her music and singing that evening, I went up to her and told her, "You have an incredible voice."

"I like you guys' stuff too," she fired back, referring to

the music that BeBe and I made together. There's so much jealousy, competition, and anxiety in the music industry, especially between women, that it surprised both of us, I suppose, that we could genuinely compliment each other. Later that night, she surprised BeBe and me by coming to a show of ours at Concert by the Seas wrapped in a fur, and ended up onstage with us, singing with us—outsinging us in fact—on our own songs. The energy was right, the music was right, the friendship was right, and it was instantaneous.

After the performance I teased her and said, "Okay, you can go home now with that beautiful voice of yours, so we can keep our jobs." The girl blows me away with her vocal power and tones. She has the ability to hold a note until she falls out, and then she has the soul as well. The first time a friend first shared a Whitney Houston tape with me, she said, "There's someone singing who sounds just like you." Once I heard Whitney singing "Saving All My Love for You," I said to myself, "Oh yeah, right. In *heaven*, I'm going to sound like that!"

That night was the start of a wonderful friendship marked by visits, phone calls, laughter, cheering for each other, and praying for each other and has lasted for more than ten years. Whitney and I are like sisters. She's one of the family now. BeBe produced the song "Jesus Loves Me" on her Grammy-winning multimillion-selling soundtrack for *The Bodyguard*, and my brother Marvin was the minister at her wedding. People are surprised by our friendship but shouldn't be. We have a lot in common. Both of us grew up in the church and got our start there singing in the church choir. We're only a year apart. She's the big sister I never had, although I grew up in a big family, and there's only Whitney and her two brothers. We're both homebodies, and we are both daughters of singing mothers, although Whitney's mother achieved her fame when she was young singing with the soul group Sweet Inspiration. In fact, both sets of parents played an integral part in our growing up in the music industry and were constantly consulted in our careers.

The biggest secret of all is that Whitney is really a very down-to-earth sister which no one believes with all her fame and fortune. Best of all, I knew I'd found my sister soul mate when I saw how much the girl perspires when she sings. "Now *this* is my sister!" I said when I noticed her reaching for handkerchiefs and tissues and wiping her face repeatedly throughout her performance. I knew right then that Nip (her pet name among family and special friends) and I would be great friends. For the longest time, I thought I was the only female entertainer in the industry who perspires profusely when she sings! Boy, was I glad to find out that I was not alone.

Years later when we teamed up at the second annual VH 1 Honors at the Shrine Auditorium in Los Angeles, we both reached back and pulled up our church training and sang

"Bridge over Troubled Waters." It was a powerful performance, and both of us were drenched with perspiration afterward.

When I came into Whitney's life she had very few friends in the industry. But Whitney's a person just like me who wants the same things as the rest of us. When we visited her new house in New Jersey later that year on Thanksgiving and saw how excited she was to have BeBe and me there and how excited she was to show us around, I chided her, "Girlfriend, have you had anyone else to your house?" She cracked up. "I guess it's obvious, huh?" she said. The girl was excited to have friends over.

Until I met Whitney I didn't know how much I did not want to be famous. She has to worry about people with cameras in her front yard and backyard. I don't know how she deals with it. I'm not worrying about anyone in my backyard with a camera. "Thank God," I tease her. "I don't know how much longer I can be your friend because you're going to have me tearing down newspaper racks." Every time I see how the tabloids spread lies about her I want to explode. I get an attitude.

"I'm sick of seeing your face on tabloids," I tell her whenever we begin a conversation. The time that hurt most was when she was pregnant with my goddaughter Bobbi Kristina and friends in New Jersey threw a big baby shower for her. Everyone at the house was family and friends. It was supposed to be private. Some weeks later I was in the grocery store and a picture from Whitney's shower shows up on the cover of a tabloid with some ridiculous headline about her being obese. "Who would sell her out like this!" I screamed at no one. I was floored. I wanted to cry, but I had to pull myself together. The only thing I could come up with was that when the pictures were being developed, maybe someone at the lab made a copy of one of the pictures. You don't want to think that one of the people you let in your home might have sold you out, but that's the kind of stuff my friend has to deal with all of the time. Everybody is pulling on her, and everybody wants something from her because of who she is. I didn't want my friend to see that picture, and I wished I could pay someone to burn every copy of that tabloid that week. I wanted so badly to spare her that pain. Being friends with Whitney has taught me a lot: you can be the biggest female artist in the world and still be kind, down-to-earth, and have a warm heart. Whitney is a jewel, but I am convinced from watching all that she has endured in this industry that I never want to be that famous.

An interviewer once asked, "CeCe, what does Whitney have that you want? Whitney, what does CeCe have that you want?" We burst out laughing at the same time. That's not what our relationship is about. But we were good-natured. Whitney spoke up first, "CeCe doesn't want anything."

I chuckled, "Shut up, girl."

"You know it's true. You don't want *anything*."

I answered, "Look now, if I could eat anything and remain a size four, I would be delighted," I blurted out.

Our schedules are hectic, and our obligations to our families and careers prevent us from talking on the telephone as much as other girlfriends, but you don't have to talk to your real friend often in order to be friends. When we talk, however infrequently, we just pick up where we left off. If things are particularly rough in our lives at the time, we've covenanted to call no matter how far away, no matter what time of the day, no matter what the other is doing. That's what friends are for. That day when Whitney and I sang "Count on Me" for her *Waiting to Exhale* soundtrack, I knew our sister covenant was for real. The energy we shared singing that song together that day in the studio comes through, and I believe that explains why the song scored as a Top Ten on the pop charts and number one on *Billboard*'s R & B charts shortly after its release.

❧ ❧

I've learned that stardom can isolate you and insulate you from good friendships. I look around at some of the bad choices, ugly attitudes, and competitive streaks of others in the field and I see how the desperate wish to be a star can also insulate you from good, sound, sisterly advice. I never want to get so competitive and consumed with myself and my image that no one cares enough to reach out to me to tell me the truth.

Family sees to it you don't lose contact with the truth. When I receive criticism from someone I love and respect, I listen to it and pray about it. If the criticism is from someone unknown or suspicious, I pray about it. When I look at my background, I realize God knew what He was preparing for us. All those years being a Holy Roller in school taught me how to stand alone, how not to be afraid to be different. Now, I try to be sure to keep myself with family and close friends who I know love me enough to tell me the truth. Those times when I'm tempted to compare myself to other singers who are better singers, more beautiful, more successful, and more famous, I hear my parents' words, "Just be yourself. Be what God has called you to be."

Follow the Spirit

Follow the spirit
and you will never lose your way,
for the spirit knows from day to day
what you should do and what you should say.
The holy spirit is our friend,
always there to lead and guide;
it never makes mistakes;
it's the spirit of truth so it can't lie.

Follow the spirit,
let nothing distract;
you will have an abundance
and you will never lack.
Understanding, wisdom and knowledge
are what you will gain,
for the Spirit is a teacher
and will instruct you until the end.

11

The Power of Prayer

The effective, fervent prayer of a righteous man
avails much.
—James 5:16

$\mathcal{P}$eople look at my life and think of me as blessed. I am blessed, but not in the way they think. Being blessed has nothing to do with the fame, the recognition, the awards, or the money that I've achieved during my short lifetime as a performing artist. Being blessed is knowing God, knowing who you are and what your purpose is. That's the true blessing. Certainly, I am blessed to have been raised in a family that instilled in me at an early age a strong sense of *somebodyness*, a family that provided me with the opportunities to discover my talents and find my direction.

I'm glad my parents and talented siblings made me join them around the family piano when I was a little girl. I'm grateful to Sister Joyce Glenn for making me sing my first solo at a young age at the August convocation. God has used these wonderful events in my life to bless me with a career that now at thirty-four years old has surpassed my wildest imaginings.

Being blessed with success, however, has not exempted me from sorrow and disappointments.

Life makes certain that irrespective of our station in life we will all have our share of heartbreaks. I have always presented myself as the girl next door because that's who I am. I don't feel that I'm any better than anyone else, and I have never wanted people to think of me as anything other. I never wanted to be a performer who uses her personal tragedies to gain publicity for her music. But performers are human too, however, and people need to know that. We go through hurt, we go through pain, and we get songs through experiences. As we reveal these things, people are touched. God let me know it's okay to be human, and it's okay to let people see that we're able to minister in song *because* we've lived through real-life experiences. There's a difference between exploiting my hurts to fuel my career and sharing my hurts so that others might understand the character of my walk with God.

There is a story in the Bible where one of Jesus' disciples, after being told by the other disciples that Jesus had been raised from the dead, refused to believe their report, saying that not until he touched the wounds himself on Jesus' scarred body would he believe that the man they'd seen was really Jesus. Sometimes, it's only when you open up and show some of your scars that people know you are really human. Until now, I have let my music communicate how I've felt in my heart. But sometimes the story behind the music can be as important as the story told by the music.

Of all the songs that BeBe and I sang during our career, one ballad in particular has come to have a very special meaning in my life.

When I arrived in New York to join BeBe in the studio to record the song, I was met with some harrowing news. I discovered that BeBe, who had already been in New York a few days working on the song, had been rushed to Mt. Sinai Hospital. My heart fainted inside when I heard the word *hospital*. "Rushed to the hospital?" I remember saying, dread rising in me. "What's going on? What's going on with my brother?" I wanted to know. None of the musicians and producers who had been working with him there in the studio in New York knew at the time what was wrong with BeBe. They just knew that he'd been complaining of some pain all morning long and had become violently ill later in the day.

I was a wreck during the drive to the hospital. My mind was racing. I couldn't imagine life without BeBe. "No please, Lord," I kept praying, "not BeBe. Not my brother." My mind was racing with possibilities and inevitabilities as I dialed the string of numbers given to me. "This is too much, Lord," I kept saying. "I can't do this. If anything happens to my brother . . ." I couldn't finish the sentence as I tried in vain to reach my brother by phone in the car. Each thought in my mind was more dreaded than the one before. The words "If anything happens to my brother . . ." kept ringing in my ears.

BeBe knew even in his sickness that he had to get to me. He knew I'd be a total wreck not knowing his condition. When I was finally able to reach him, I told him that I was on my way to the hospital, but he begged me not to come. "No, CeCe, don't come. I'm fine."

BeBe's appendix had ruptured, and he needed emergency surgery. BeBe was more worried about the fact that we had a recording deadline to make. "Just how am I supposed to sing 'If Anything Ever Happened To You,' knowing you're lying somewhere on a gurney in a hospital?" I shot back. But BeBe begged me to go on with the song, and I did—singing and praying the entire time.

Illness, whether it's yours or someone else's, has the power to bring you to your senses. It causes you to rethink what it means to be blessed. You find yourself rethinking what it means to live. Standing in the studio alone without my brother, uncertain about how he was faring under a surgeon's knife, I knew instinctively that part of what it meant for me at that moment to be blessed was to have the chance to collaborate and work closely with someone special for the greater part of my life, someone I trusted and loved, in this case my own brother. Even though BeBe and I are as different as night and day and have had our creative, professional, and sibling differences, we're still family. Despite finally settling down and marrying a wonderful girl name Debbie Johnson, who looks just like my mother, BeBe still remained a go-getter. He was still experimenting with new sounds and creative possibilities. He was still always ready to go when I was ready to stay home. He loved to travel and didn't mind booking after booking, even though I was clamoring for downtime, preferring to be home with my family than on some tour bus on a remote road in Texas. Nevertheless, we'd been singing together since we were kids and were for all practical purposes glued at the hip. We grew up in the business together. "Lord, BeBe is my partner for life," I recall thinking as I positioned the headphones on my ears and whispered a prayer for the brother two years older than me. I whispered that prayer and sang "If Anything Ever Happened to You," praying and thanking God for my brother's life.

I heard a preacher once say: faith is developed in the dark. You can't explain why things happen the way they do. You can't know how things will wind up. You don't know how long it will be dark. But you know that if you can just manage to stand, believing and trusting, there *will* be light after the darkness. I have had my share of dark days—in my career, in my relationships with my siblings, in my marriage, with my children, in my soul, and in my faith. It was all I could do to fumble around the floor, through the strewn debris, and grope for a door handle, a window ledge, a light switch, something to help me make out my way. I've always known the only way to make it through any situation was through God's word. It's a lamp for the feet and a light for the path. I pray to stay focused, and I pray—the old-fashioned way. I get down on my hands and knees at the side of my bed, and I read my Bible. When life knocks me on my backside and leaves me spiritually numb and dazed such that I can't find the words to pray, I dial up my church family to pray for me.

"The effectual, fervent prayers of the righteous availeth much," says the Bible. From as far back as the days when I was growing up in the church and heard adults in the church testifying about the power of prayer, watched members of the church stream up to the altar during prayer time, and observed the elders of the church coming over to the house and praying with my Mom and Dad, I have always believed in the power of prayer. Better yet, my husband and I have seen to it that no matter where we go, our family stays close to *one* of the most important lifelines in prayer: the church. When Alvin and I decided in 1989 to move the family to Nashville, where my record company, producers, and much of my business in the industry took place, and where BeBe had moved a year earlier with Debbie, one of the first things we did when we arrived was find a church where the family could worship together. I was glad we did when another storm emerged on the horizon some years later in the form of another illness within my family. You can never have too many people praying for you.

✹ ✹

My brother Ronald's illness knocked our family to its knees. BeBe's ruptured appendix scared us, but Ronald's ruptured heart on the operating table tested us. It was the greatest test of our family's faith, love and unity, and it was also the darkest period of my life. I didn't understand what God was doing. How do you explain an event as being both the darkest and the brightest in your life, one that both shatters your faith and strengthens your faith at the same time? I am convinced that our family could not have survived the trauma of watching Ronald's life hang in the balance had we not had church families across the country praying and interceding to God on our behalf.

When the word got out that Ronald was in a Michigan hospital facing emergency heart surgery, churches all over the country where either The Winans had performed or where BeBe and I had performed during our careers stopped to pray for Ronald Winans. Baptists, Methodists, Presbyterians, Episcopalians, Catholics, Nazarenes, Pentecostals, Adventists, and those in nondenominational services, seekers of all colors, raised their voice in unity on my brother's behalf.

It was heartening to see and feel the warmth and love of God's people we had ministered to through song over the years now graciously carry us in prayer as we struggled to find the words to pray for ourselves. How comforting it was to know that across the country a great chain of prayer warriors were phoning, leaving messages, sending telegrams, and having prayer meetings on behalf of Ronald as he lay near death in an Ann Arbor hospital.

I have seven brothers and two sisters, and each one of my siblings is very special to me. I can't imagine life without any of them. Even though we're not a very demonstrative bunch, and until then we had found it nearly impossible to find a time when we all could make it back to Mom and Dad's for family gatherings given our careers and family responsibilities, Ronald's illness proved that when there's a crisis in any of our lives, everyone will stop what he or she is doing to come home.

The experience of almost losing Ronald changed me. I can never go back to the person I was before. Before his illness and BeBe's, I'd never given my family's mortality enough thought. Fortunately, our family has remained a relatively young, healthy lot, but it seems in the middle of the 1990s that within a span of four years, with sickness upon sickness, we began to be reminded of just how brief life can be. It was as though God was tapping the family on the shoulders and reminding us against becoming so enamored of our professional responsibilities that we neglected to spend time with family. I for one do not want to look around one day and discover that I had let time slip away and had failed to show my family how much they mean to me. It's important to communicate how much you love one another while there's still opportunity because life may not permit you the opportunity to say good-bye.

It remains a mystery to his doctors how Ronald managed to walk into the hospital upright and conscious. Marvin had driven Ronald to the hospital because he had been complaining all morning of a shortness of breath and was coughing. Upon examination, the doctors discovered that Ronald had had a major heart attack months before and didn't know it. That morning, his poor heart was showing the telltale signs of weakness and deterioration. After a heart specialist was brought in to examine Ronald, Marvin was advised to phone the whole family.

As fate would have it I was on location in Salt Lake City, Utah, waiting to be called up for a brief cameo appearance on the television show *Touched By an Angel*. I was scheduled to be out there for three days. The phone call about Ronald's condition came in on day number one. The call reached me just as I was waiting to be fitted in costume. I dropped everything and made reservations to leave on the first plane to Detroit. If anyone needed an angel, I reasoned, Ronald was the one. I dashed to join my brother's side there in Detroit with the rest of my family. Sometimes the best thing we can do is to stand at the bedside praying for the infirm until the angel of the Lord is manifested. On the plane from Salt Lake City to Detroit, the fear rising up in me was déjà vu. "This isn't supposed to happen," I prayed. "Not now. No, God, not Ronald." My mind kept retracing special memories of Ronald, extending all the way to the days when we were young. Ronald was the one who played with me when I was a little girl, taught me how to color my dolls' hair, combed and styled my own hair for me, and protected me from time to time from the bullying of the others. He has always been the big teddy bear of the family, the nurturer, the softer soul, the one most likely to dash to the defense of everyone and to protect everyone else. "No, God, not Ronald," I implored on the plane.

We all flew in. After all, my brother's life was hanging in the balance. I can never forget the look on the doctors' faces when after consulting among themselves they turned to the family and informed us that there was nothing they could do to save my brother. Ronald was going to die, one of them said, repeating the words several times in the hopes of getting through the stunned looks on our faces. One doctor suggested that we wake Ronald up to say our good-byes. Everyone gasped. Slowly, as the words began to sink in, tears began to make their way down each of our faces. Several of my big robust brothers who are normally macho and tough cried as well. Mom and Dad clung to each other and buried their faces in each other's shoulders. I was too stunned to know how to respond. My sister Angie lost it. The girl in the family with the feisty and mercurial temperament, Angie could be counted on to gather her senses and pitch a fit. She shouted at the doctors, "He's not. He's not going to die. My brother is not going to die!" Angie's heart was insulted by the doctors' prognosis. I pulled her aside later on when we were alone, teasing her. "Girl, how can you go off like that in the name of the Lord?" We laugh about that now.

The family began to pray and called everyone we knew who knew how to pray and asked them to pray. We sang and we prayed. I could taste the fear creeping up into my throat. My mouth grew dry when I saw Mom. How many times had I looked to this woman for faith? How many times had I drawn strength from her and let her normally calm gentle reactions become a gauge for my own reaction? How many times had I been comforted by her words "The Lord will make a way somehow." Now she stood crying at the bedside of her second oldest son. She was lost in her own world of private memories. Fortunately Elder Stacks, our pastor, was there with us and began to encourage us to keep the faith. He admonished us to join him around my brother's bed. We prayed in Ronald's hospital room. We also sang. We weren't singing for fame and fortune. We were singing for the life of one of our own.

The next day the doctor returned after more consultation to say that he wanted to modify his early prognosis, and *perhaps* Ronald had a fifty-fifty chance. After much prayer and consultation of our own, we decided to take our chances with the operation. We consented to let the doctor begin the work to repair Ronald's aorta. Before the operation we ran into an old church friend, Cory Jackson, who was working there at the hospital. His job allowed him to go into the operating room with Ronald and observe. He would be the one to come in and out of the operating room to tell us what to pray.

It's the most incredible feeling in the world—to be surrounded in prayer. We could feel the prayers. I don't know how families without faith, how other people go through crises without this host of prayer warriors. We took shifts all night long before the operation. Singing over him and anointing him with oil, praying around his bed, and speaking words of encouragement into his ear were incredible experiences. It was such a wonderful thing for our children to experience. Alvin and Ashley, along with their many cousins, had a chance to watch their parents huddling together in prayer. They saw us pulling together. I will never be the same again. The words to one of Andrae Crouch's songs comes to mind about the lessons that problems teach us, such as learning to trust Jesus and learning that there is no problem too difficult for God. Through it all, I have learned some things about the Lord.

For a time there it felt like warfare. I could feel the spiritual warfare. We couldn't think about death. We refused to entertain the thought of death. We were warring with demonic forces for my brother's life. Because of our experience there at

Ronald's bedside, I am convinced there is power in family and the devil knows that. We were fighting for my brother's life with the only thing that we knew worked, namely prayer and pleading the blood of Jesus over him. It was such a team effort.

When you're in trouble, you just learn how much you need others. From the janitors at the hospital to the people who worked in admissions, people dropped in to encourage our hearts. Friends came in from all over to take turns sitting with the family. Cards and telegrams flooded the hospital. Hospital staff who knew our family, had heard us in concerts, or had grown up coming to our family concerts at Mercy College took a special interest in our crisis. People brought us food, changes of clothes, and took care of our children as we waited for hours for word from the doctors. God sent angels in various forms to remind us what we already knew, namely that God had all power.

One angel in particular was a white man we got to know only as Brother Bill. Brother Bill's wife was in the hospital. My father started to go around from ward to ward, visiting with some of the ill people on the floors as a way to keep himself busy and to take his mind off the crisis with his son. When he told people that he was a minister, he prayed for those who asked him to. Brother Bill's wife was one of them. Grateful for Dad's prayer, he asked Dad why he was there. Dad told him about Ronald. "Oh, Ronald is going to be fine," Brother promptly replied. Not knowing the situation and not knowing our family, Brother Bill took it upon himself to drop by the waiting room to remind us, "You know Ronald is going to be all right." "Who is this man?" my brothers and sisters started to ask one another.

"You've got to expect a miracle in order to get one," he kept popping in and saying. Brother Bill kept coming in, almost intrusively. We all couldn't understand why he'd become attached to the plight of strangers when his own wife lay down the hall with tubes of her own.

"You don't get it unless you expect it," he came in once and said. He was like an angel. His faith was so strong for us. He shook us up and reminded us what we already knew. When you're in that situation it's so easy to forget, so easy to let go. You're always encouraging others. But when you're in that situation, you have to be reminded: don't give up. Hold on. Keep believing. Trust in God. Eventually Cory came out of the operating room, and my sister Angie noticed him talking to a member of the family. Angie read his lips, "Ronald is dead." She came over to me and whispered in my ear, "CeCe, I just saw Cory say 'Ronald is dead.'" But then she added. "We rebuke that."

"Amen," I replied.

After a few more minutes, one of the doctors operating on Ronald came down the corridor to meet with us. The expression on his face was grave. Ronald's heart had exploded on the operating table, he informed us.

"We've done all we can do, it's between God and Ronald. I'm going back here to try again. He's been dead approximately four minutes."

"Can we pray for you?" my father asked. The doctor said yes, so we prayed for him before he went back to try to revive Ronald's life. "Where is the chapel?" my brother Marvin asked. One of the nurses directed us to the chapel, and the family all marched there to gather ourselves. This time, time stood still. We knew we couldn't afford to doubt. Everything we'd been taught was on the line, and nothing else mattered. This time, the family knelt wherever we could find a cleared space and turned our face toward Jesus, begging for a miracle. We stayed like that for what seemed like hours.

Finally, my cousin Dwayne came running down the hall screaming, "Nothing but good news, nothing but good news, nothing but good news! Ronald is going to recovery. Ronald is fine." Bedlam broke out in the chapel and in the halls of the hospital. "Praise the Lord!" "Thank you, Jesus!" "Mercy!" "Glory to God!" The tears flowed down my face as I watched Mom and Dad collapse in each other's arms. Family and friends were leaping for joy, some running through the halls shouting and praising the Lord.

My brother Ronald had been raised from the dead. He went into cardiac arrest on the operating table and expired, but with God's help the doctors were able to revive him. It was a miracle. A couple of the doctors confided that they felt the presence of the divine in the room as they operated. What makes Ronald's miracle all the more special is that it was borne on the wings of prayers of not only his family, but also of people from across the country, friends and coworkers, hospital personnel, strangers in corridors, a platoon of mercy angels joining us in prayer and unity.

※ ※

A few months later, my father had to have brain surgery, if there is such a thing. My mother noticed that he didn't flinch that morning at the breakfast table when his hand touched a cup of very hot coffee. He hadn't felt anything. She thought he'd had a stroke. She noticed that he was becoming increasingly incoherent as they made their way to the hospital. The doctors did a scan and found that there was blood on the brain. Thank God, it wasn't *in* the brain—it was on his brain. I told Alvin that I had to get up to Detroit to see about my mother. I was worried that having just come through Ronald's ordeal, she might find this to be too much for her. I knew she was still exhausted and wasted by what we'd gone through with Ronald and would probably need me.

"Oh Lord, this is in Your hands," I remember saying. "If you did it for Ronald, I know you can do it for Dad." They drilled a hole in Dad's skull, drained the fluid, sewed him back up, and he was out. By the time Alvin and I arrived in Detroit, they were preparing to let Dad out of the hospital. He never missed a beat. By the time we caught up with him, he was preaching to everyone in the hospital. You'd never know that anything had happened to him, except for the little almost imperceptible scar on his head.

∾ ∾

It's one thing to hear others testify about miracles. It's another thing to experience one for yourself. When I was a child growing up in the Pentecostal church, I'd sat in the choir loft with the other young people listening to the heartrending testimonies of adults of how God had delivered them. Still there's nothing like experiencing a miracle to help you really get to know God for yourself. I remember how I, my siblings, and the rest of the youth of the church would snicker and mock the overdramatized testimonies of our elders, as youth are wont to do. When someone stood and began their oration with the typical "you-don't-know-like-I-know-what-the-Lord-has-done-for-me" introduction, we would sit up and pay attention. As children, we thought these were hilarious ways in which the adults recounted healing miracles, and supernatural interventions by God. What did we know about the things our parents needed, the things they were helpless to provide us in trying to keep us and themselves whole and alive?

What did we know about life's swift transitions?

What did we know about the vicissitudes of life, that with one phone call one's whole life can be turned upside down?

We didn't know. We were children back then, unaware of how impossible it is to witness a miracle and remain composed, unaware of the fact that just up the road, around the bend, in the fullness of time, life would have us storming the altars with our own supplications, and if we hold on to our faith, our own testimonies of deliverance.

Prayer

Prayer changes things,
when you believe.
Have faith in God's promises,
not in what you see.

Prayer changes things,
it's more powerful than any weapon,
always manifesting miracles,
carrying our petitions straight up to heaven.

Prayer changes things,
always has, and always will.
So pray without ceasing,
and you will discover the power of prayer is real.

Epilogue

Alone in His Presence

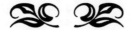

Thou will show me the path of life:
in thy presence is the fullness of joy;
at thy right hand there are pleasures for evermore.
—*Psalms 16:11*

$\mathcal{F}$aith is about how you live
your life in the meantime, how you make decisions when you
don't know for sure what's next. What you do with yourself
between the last time you heard from God and the next time
you hear from God is the ongoing challenge of a life of faith.
Despite years of criticism about the untraditional sound of our
music, our message not being Christian enough, and even our
look being too slick and sophisticated, after nine years our

music had won the respect and admiration of both those in the industry and those beyond the industry.

With five albums to our credit, BeBe and I had managed to win seven Grammy Awards, seven Dove Awards, five Stellar Awards, and three NAACP Image Awards. Almost all of our albums had songs that eventually became hits on both the R & B and Inspiration charts. We were particularly proud of the fact that our second album, *Heaven,* was the first gospel recording to reach the top ten on *Billboard*'s R & B charts since Aretha Franklin's *Amazing Grace* in 1972. One of our albums went platinum (*Different Lifestyles*) and two went gold (*Heaven* and *Relationships*). BeBe and I kept hectic schedules, traveling on concert tours, doing publicity shoots, special engagements, and interviews, working with charities, and making television guest appearances on *The Tonight Show, Live with Regis & Kathie Lee,* the 1994 Grammy Awards telecast, Fox television's *Martin, Sesame Street,* and *Showtime at the Apollo,* and other shows. Although we were grateful for all the acclaim and were excited by all the doors and opportunities that became available to us as BeBe & CeCe, we were especially proud of the fact that our songs were doing what God wanted them to do, that both core gospel fans as well as mainstream audiences found hope and inspiration in our music, and that audiences of different races and backgrounds were able to come together in love and unity under the banner of our songs. That was the confirmation to us that we had done what God wanted us to do. By 1995, after we had finished our fifth album, *Relationships,* and done the tour for the album, I knew it was time to do something different. Bebe and I both knew it. I just wasn't sure what form "different" would take.

God has always taken care of me. If you come from nothing, you know how to deal with nothing. I didn't get into this business in search of fame and fortune. I haven't been freaked out by the down times when the invitations were lean. I've just had to trust God, and trusting God has always worked for me.

My thing has always been, "If God has called me to do this, then God will just have to make a way," which takes a load off your brain. Without that assurance, this business will crush your spirits. You can make albums that never get put out. You find yourself worrying about who sings better, who's prettier, who has a hit—and these things will really mess your mind up. When you think you've got to make sure your name is being called, make sure you're at the right place at the right time, make sure you are seen, you become desperate. God has allowed me to stand back sometimes and feel the fear I would have if I weren't in Him. I would be totally lost without God.

Speaking of lost, there was a time in my life when I thought I couldn't perform if I didn't have BeBe next to me. But in 1995 God showed me differently. About that time I felt certain inside that God was bringing me into another calling, one that required me to strike out on my own, this time by myself. Neither of us believed that the duo BeBe & CeCe was over, but

I think God decided that it was time for both of us to have the opportunity to minister on another level. It's as though God had elevated us to a place of fame in our career, given us an audience, given us the respect of our peers, and now said, "I want to deal with you both individually now. I want to prepare you both for different ministries, and yet another phase of your lives." I went into the studio in 1995 to make my first recording by myself. It was not difficult to decide upon a title for my solo recording, *Alone in His Presence*.

I wanted *Alone in His Presence* to be a closer look at me without all the facade around me. I was dying to get back to some of the traditional hymns of the church, not because I disliked contemporary gospel, far from it. I was ready to get back to a part of my background that I always cherished, and I wanted desperately to share that part with the rest of the world. I thought that it was important that our generation and the generation that comes after mine realize the importance of those hymns *also* as part of the rich legacy of our ancestors. Hymns like "Amazing Grace" and "Great Is Thy Faithfulness," "I Surrender All" and "Blessed Assurance" were ones our parents drew upon during their quiet times, when they poured out their hearts to God. I have always thought it was important that young people connect with the older songs as well. I cherished these songs as ones I grew up listening to in church and had drawn strength from them down through the years in my own moments of private reflection.

Definitely the highlight of the album for me was getting to sing "Great Is Thy Faithfulness" with my mom. It's because of God's faithfulness to her and her faithfulness to God that I'm as strong as I am in the faith. I knew how much that hymn meant to her, and I was looking forward to getting her into the studio to record it with me. Now I don't know if I'll invite her back, I always tease her, because she just outdid me on the whole song! When I listened back to the song, I thought to myself, "Man, I feel like such a kid next to her!"

Of course, I wouldn't be a Winans if I hadn't continued the tradition of risk taking, in this case, jazzing up a hallowed hymn of the church. Cedric and Victor Caldwell, my producers, begged me to allow them to spice up "Blessed Assurance." I was nervous about the possibility, but even I was not prepared for their spicy reinterpretation of what has to be one of the most widely regarded hymns of the church. Even nonbelievers have been known to shed a tear singing "Blessing Assurance"! When I heard Cedric and Victor's big-band jazz reinterpretation, I nearly fell over. "Look guys," I said, "if everybody loves it you guys will get all the credit, but if everybody hates it you guys will get the blame." But Cedric and Victor prevailed on me. I'm glad they did. That cut helps in giving the recording of otherwise traditional songs a real upbeat, joyful, and different sound.

❧ ❧

Going out on your own as a solo artist needn't mean going all out by yourself—severing all ties with family and trusted associates. When it was time to strike out I knew who to call on to help me get launched, the very ones who'd been my greatest fans and prayer partners throughout my career: my family! I had Mom join me on "Great Is Thy Faithfulness," Marvin wrote "Every Time," my sisters Angie and Debbie helped to sing background on a number of the songs, Ronald helped to produce some vocals, and Cedric Caldwell, my producer, is my sister Angie's husband. There is no denying, however, that when the time came for me to step from behind the curtain and walk out onstage in Sacramento, California, to sing and carry the full concert by myself I was terrified. I was weepy. I missed my brother. I was afraid I would forget my cues as I'd done so many times in the past. I didn't have anyone else's eyes on the stage to turn to see how I was doing. "Oh, BeBe, I miss you," I remember thinking. "You're not alone," God whispered in my soul. He was with me. There were Alvin's eyes staring back at me from the audience—my husband, now my personal manager, my best friend—cheering me, loving me, encouraging me, praying for me. There was the music my family had helped to create all around me as I transitioned from one song to another. And there was the peace of God that passes all understanding sweeping over my heart as I opened my mouth.

I admit that I don't know what God is up to—I never have—it was never my intention to become a singer and performer. But in all that I've done I have tried to live my life so that God could use me. And I know God has used not only me but also my entire family. I think we've made a difference. Contemporary gospel music is an exciting place to do ministry these days. It has gone into places and reached people who industry experts thought impossible to reach fifteen years ago. Improvement in the production quality of the music, more upscale marketing and packaging of the artists and their albums, and better distribution have all helped to make contemporary gospel music the fastest growing genre and the sixth most popular form of music, beating out jazz and classical. Though I'm only thirty-four years old, I tend to think that I, along with my brother BeBe and the rest of the Winans have played our part in helping to broaden people's perspective about what inspirational music can be.

When I listen to music by successful gospel artists I'm proud of the role my family played in proving that gospel could successfully compete with other musical genres for radio air play and sales.

I think of the artists who performed in the halcyon days of traditional gospel music, artists my parents grew up listening to—Sensational Nightingales, Swan Silvertones, Mighty Clouds of Joy, Gospel Harmonettes, Davis Sisters, Ward Singers, Staple Singers, Mahalia Jackson—and I pray that they are proud of the accomplishments of my generation.

I got a chance to discover firsthand how much I owe to that generation of singers when I had the chance to join the indefatigable First Lady of Gospel, Ms. Shirley Caesar, off Broadway in a play *Born to Sing*, which was written by Vy Higgensen. Every night Shirley Caesar sang me under the stage and sent me back exhausted and limping to my dressing room with her energy. She taught me a lot over the years and during that play about how to be both a woman and strong and graceful at the same time. Those of us in contemporary gospel have built on the legacy of these gospel greats, and we benefited from their sacrifices. They rode for hours, sometimes days, crowded six and eight in rundown cars, trying to get from singing engagement to singing engagement, sleeping in church members' homes, because they weren't allowed in downtown hotels. They completed sold-out performances only to find themselves having to return home more broke than they were before they left, because promoters had skipped town without paying them a dime. They sang for the sheer pleasure of glorifying God, but they also sang fully expecting to be paid for their work. They kept their menial weekday jobs so as to be free enough to minister in song to downtrodden, working-class colored people in need of inspiration and hope. They never dreamed that their sacrifices would be my inspiration.

When in 1996 I became the first black woman to win the Dove Award's "Best Female Vocal Artist" I walked onstage and accepted my award for the many women who came before me.

I wanted to be able to walk through every door God opened with integrity. It's because of God that everything has happened. He took our talents, simply because we said yes, and made us who we are today. I know if I continue to trust the Lord, everything is going to be all right. That doesn't excuse me from having to do my part. I've had to learn to stand up, speak up, and take care of business. A woman who stands up for her rights and who has opinions about how she wants to sing a song is considered difficult. Sometimes a man who speaks his mind is considered to be a man who knows what he wants and is confident and self-assured. But I like the new me, the other side of CeCe, the woman I have become at thirty-four years old. People change.

❧ ❧

Change is what I have been looking for in recent years. The older I become the more concerned I am about doing work that makes a difference in the lives of others. Music is just one of the ways I want to touch the world. Lately I've joined forces with friends to help impact the lives of teenage girls who are in dire need of a safe place to talk, dream, and be girls. The program is called My Sister's Keeper. I also do work associated with the alarming rise in the suicide rate among teenagers. I remember being a teenager. I remember feeling scared, alone, lost, and vulnerable. I also remember what it was like to have role models, schoolteachers, a church family to turn to for guidance and direction.

My second solo recording, *Everlasting Love*, is all-the-way urban inspiration, filled with contemporary hip-hop, R & B sounds as my way of reaching the world. Instead of asking them to come over to where I was and embrace my sound, I wanted to reach them by embracing their sound. I wanted to show them that being Christian and living a positive life are not boring. It's the best life because it's filled with God's pleasure, lots of laughter, and no hangovers!! I'm older now. These days I use my fame to fuel my ministry. After all these years in the business I can stretch. I've gotten to the point where I'm ready to go into warfare for the Lord.

If other entertainers can get up there and curse and take their clothes off and not care about the children, then I can use my rhythms, whichever ones suit my target audience, to stand up for the Lord.

Many times I still feel out of place and would rather be home with my family. But only in looking back and seeing how far I have come can I now see all the ways, both large and small, that God has orchestrated the events of my life.

My whole life is good, despite all the ups and downs. It always has been. I've grown up. I'm both the shy, quiet girl from Detroit who had to be forced into the limelight to sing her first solo, and I am a performer making decisions about her career, negotiating with industry heads who is unafraid to say no. At first I shied away from the limelight and didn't want to be out front. Every time I sang, I had to be pushed to do it, and every year I cried when the time came for me to sing "Fill My Cup, Lord." Now I'm glad my family and friends pushed me. I'm glad they pushed me into my purpose. I discovered that God had a call on my life, and what God was calling me to had nothing to do with becoming famous, or signing record contracts, or getting rich. That call had to do with spreading the news of the reality of God. Every year "Fill My Cup" became more and more real to me until slowly, gradually, God healed me of my fears. He used music to do it.

I have grown to appreciate the words to the song,

Fill My Cup, Lord.
I lift it up, Lord.
Come and fill this thirsting of my soul . . .

This searching, thirsting, longing for something satisfying, positive, soul quenching, something sacred is who I have always been about, and nothing that I will ever sing will go against that. My only desire always has been and will always be to please God and to be filled with His presence.

Your Presence

In your presence there's fullness of joy,
when I'm close to You I'm safe and secure.
Under the shadow of your wings I'm strong and
*   confident*
because You're faithful and true.

You are my source
You're everything I need;
with your voice and your words,
my hungry soul You feed.
When I enter your presence
I never come out the same;
great things always happen
because of the power of your name.

Sharing the Vision, Inc. is a 501-(C) (3) nonprofit organization founded by CeCe Winans in 1995. In an attempt to counteract the negative influences of our generation, we offer the following programs: My Sister's Keeper, which provides weekly support groups for young women ages 13 to 30, offers mentoring, community outreach, and positive social activities; Teen Save, which is a suicide prevention and community awareness program; and Camp CeCe, a Christian Youth Camp. For more information, please contact:

Sharing the Vision, Inc.
P.O. Box 271455
Nashville, TN 37227-1455
(615) 595-9141
Executive Director: Yolanda Shields

Check us out on our web site at
http://www.sharingthevision.org
Or E-mail us at: info@sharingthevision.org